19

# FAMOUS
# SCOTTISH
# BATTLES

# Philip Warner

# FAMOUS SCOTTISH BATTLES

*Where battles were fought*
*Why they were fought*
*How they were won and lost*

LEO COOPER
LONDON

0674I7240

# SYSTEM COPY

*The maps in this book are based upon the*
*Ordinance Survey map with the sanction of*
*the Controller of H.M. Stationery Office,*
*Crown Copyright Reserved.*

First published by Osprey Publishing Ltd.
as *British Battlefields:*
*Scotland and the Border.*

This edition published in
Great Britain in 1995 by
LEO COOPER
190 Shaftesbury Avenue, London WC2H 8JL
an imprint of
Pen & Sword Books Ltd,
47 Church Street
Barnsley, South Yorkshire S70 2AS

Text © Philip Warner, 1975, 1995


A CIP record for this book is available from the British Library

ISBN 0-85052-487-3

Printed and bound in the United States of America

# CONTENTS

List of maps                                          7

Note on map references                               12

Introduction                                         13

The Battles:

Stirling Bridge 1297                                 47

Falkirk 1298                                         53

Bannockburn 1314                                     59

Halidon Hill 1333                                    69

Neville's Cross 1346                                 73

Homildon Hill 1402                                   81

An Interim of Anarchy and Border Warfare             87

Ancrum Moor 1545                                     99

Pinkie 1547                                         105

Newburn 1640                                        113

Kilsyth 1645                                        117

Philiphaugh 1645                                    121

Dunbar 1650                                         125

Killiecrankie 1689                              129

Glencoe 1692                                    137

Prestonpans 1745                                141

Culloden 1746                                   149


Index                                           157

# THE MAPS

*with grid references and directions*
*(between pages 80 and 81)*

1¹/₄ inches to 1 mile     2 cm to 1 km     1:50,000

*Road numbers are accurate at the time of writing. Although renumbering does*
*sometime occur, visitors using the maps should have no difficulty in finding*
*the battlefields.*

## I STIRLING BRIDGE

**O.S. Map no. 57 (Stirling and The Trossachs Area) grid reference 784 951.** The original bridge has now disappeared but the later, nearby, footbridge gives a good idea of its type. Note the width and speed of the river. A good idea of the tactical situation may be gained from looking over the castle ramparts or from the Wallace Monument.

## II FALKIRK

**O.S. Map no. 65 (Falkirk and West Lothian) grid reference 885 796.** This site is often confused with that of the 1746 battle (a Jacobite victory) which took place two miles southeast of the town, where there is a monument near Greenbank. The 1298 battle took place in the middle of the town on land which has now been built over, but in spite of the bricks and mortar and roads it is still possible to obtain a fair view of the lie of the land. The Wallace Street and Thornhill Road intersection is thought to be the centre of the battlefield.

## III BANNOCKBURN

**O.S. Map no. 57 (Stirling and The Trossachs Area) grid reference 793 905.** Take the A872 south from Stirling. One mile along you come to 50 acres of National Trust for Scotland property with a Heritage centre, bookshop, restaurant and diorama. The statue of Bruce, set up in 1964, probably marks the spot where he stood to observe the advancing English army: the battlefield extended south and east of this position. The pits, south and east of the Borestone, reopened in the 19th century, were only eighteen inches deep but contained sharp hazel stakes.

## IV HALIDON HILL

**O.S. Map no. 75 (Berwick-upon-Tweed) grid reference 968 547.** The battlefield is ten miles out of Berwick along the A6105. There is a monument, half-concealed in the hedge, on the northern side of the road. Easily seen. No visitor should omit to take a good long look at Berwick, inspect the ruined castle and visit the museum. Peaceful today, but once a scene of frequent warfare.

## V NEVILLE'S CROSS

**O.S. Map no. 88 (Tyneside and Durham) grid reference 264 427.** Although much built over, this site is not difficult to visualize. Take the point where the A167 crosses the railway line and you are in the centre of the beginning of the battle. Move to Red Hills and you are in the final stages. Flass Bog was to the northeast of Robert's position.

## VI HOMILDON HILL

**O.S. Map no. 75 (Berwick-upon-Tweed) grid reference 970 296.** This is easy to find as it is two miles west of Wooler, though it is now usually called Humbleton. The Bendar stone is in the middle of a field by the side of the road and easily viewable. Red Riggs is a few hundred yards to the southeast. A rigg was an old English ridge.

## VII ANCRUM MOOR

**O.S. Map no. 74 (Kelso and surrounding area) grid reference 619 273.** The battlefield is four miles northwest of Jedburgh and some way from Ancrum itself. Some early accounts of this battle place it around Reniel Heugh (two miles northwest), which has Iron Age forts and was no doubt the scene of battles but not this one.

## VIII PINKIE

**O.S. Map no. 66 (Edinburgh and Midlothian Area) grid reference 362 716.** Easily seen. Note the vulnerability of the Scots to a bombardment from the sea. The little Pinkie burn, opposite Loretto, became choked with bodies and a major hazard, as small streams often did on battlefields.

## IX NEWBURN

**O.S. Map no. 88 (Tyneside and Durham Area) grid reference 165 653.** The battle was by Newburn bridge. Note the church tower from which Leslie fired his cannon.

## X KILSYTH

**O.S. Map no. 64 (Glasgow) grid reference 740 786.** Take the A803 out of Kilsyth. Turn left into the grounds of Colzium House (now a Community Centre). In front of the house you will see the Montrose memorial. The battlefield area is to the east: some of it is now covered by an artificial lake. Relics occasionally come to light. As you look at the terrain you will probably be as surprised as Montrose was that he was offered battle here.

## XI PHILIPHAUGH

**O.S. Map no. 73 (Peebles, Galashiels) grid reference 456 284.** Take the A707 south from Selkirk. Turn left to the A708. Philiphaugh Farm is on the immediate right of this junction: the rest of the battlefield is to your left and ahead of you. Newark Castle is two miles further along and may be seen from the road.

## XII DUNBAR

**O.S. Map no. 67 (Duns, Dunbar and Eyemouth) grid reference 704 768.** Take the A1087 south of Dunbar. Look for the cement works on your left: there is a plaque at the turning. The above map reference gives the final position of Leslie's right wing before it disintegrated. Interesting harbour and castle ruins.

## XIII KILLIECRANKIE

**O.S. Map no. 43 (Braemar to Blair Atholl) grid reference 912 628.** The A9 runs through the pass and takes you by the National Trust for Scotland Centre, which has an interesting diorama of the battle. Look up the slope past Urrard House to appreciate Mackay's position. The Soldier's Leap is also clearly marked.

# XIV GLENCOE

**O.S. Map no. 41 (Ben Nevis and Fort William) grid reference 148 559.** The A82 passes through the glen on the way up to Oban. The scene of the massacre—as far as is known—is on the northern slope of Aonach Dubh, south of the river Coe. Audio-visual display in the National Trust for Scotland Centre. Walkers exploring the surrounding area should be aware of the hazards: there have been many accidents.

# XV PRESTONPANS

**O.S. Map no. 66 (Edinburgh and Midlothian Area) grid reference 396 745.** The map reference covers the centre of the approximate battlefield, but it extended over a wide area. Take the A1 from Edinburgh, then turn left along the A198. Ignore all signs directing to Prestonpans itself. Monuments to Gardiner and the 1745. Follow the Scottish charge from Riggonhead.

# XVI CULLODEN

**O.S. Map no. 27 (Nairn, Forres and Surrounding Area) grid reference 736 452** Take the A9 from Inverness: turn left on to the B9006 and seven miles from Inverness you may see the battlefield on each side of this road. The mass graves are marked by mounds and headstones. The site is in the excellent care of the National Trust for Scotland and there is a good visitors' centre where there is a bookshop, restaurant and video cinema which depicts the reason for, course of, and aftermath of the battle. Signs on the field show where the regiments fought.

## Note on map references

All Ordnance Survey maps are overlaid with an arrangement of numbered lines called the grid system, which enables any point on a map to be easily and accurately identified.

A map reference is given in two sets of three figures, for example 396 112. The first two figures of each trio (39 and 11) are the vertical line (northings) and the horizontal line (eastings) respectively; they intersect in the south-west (bottom left) corner of the square to which they refer. Smaller divisions of the square are not marked but may be estimated, and the third figures of each trio (6 and 2) represent the 'tenths' of the lines east and north (right and upwards). Thus 396 112 indicates a point six-tenths east and two-tenths north of the intersection of northing 39 and easting 11.

As the side of a square represents one kilometre (1,000 metres) a tenth of that line must represent 100 metres: thus map references are correct to 100 metres.

# INTRODUCTION

There is a widespread belief that England and Scotland fought ferociously in time of war but that otherwise there was peace in the north. This is far from the truth. For centuries, families from either country would make forays across the border. When such raids became too continuous, too destructive, and too successful, a whole district would rise in arms and make a punitive reprisal. Nobody expected – or would have wished – otherwise. These activities stemmed not so much from greed, aggression, or patriotism, as from boredom and lack of leisure-time pursuits. There was seldom peace in the north and the result of this was that, when full-scale war came, there were abundant supplies of hardened fighting men to draw on. They did not, in those early days, care to travel too far from home and there was a tendency to leave early in a campaign with a good share of plunder. But, while they were fighting, they were not usually stopped while there was life in their bodies.

Nor was fighting always across the border. The 'other country' was always there but in one's own – on either side of the border – there were plenty of old and new scores to settle. Every family, every tribe, and every clan had a hated rival and opponent. In fact it was easier to fight one's neighbour than a foreigner; one had no particular grudge against the men one had never seen, but a neighbour or a kinsman – that was a different story.

In consequence, the borderers, whether English or Scottish, acquired over the centuries a formidable fighting reputation.

They were not, it will be freely acknowledged, necessarily better than men from other parts of the British Isles but they were certainly as good. Furthermore, they were remarkably consistent. Nowadays, in their wisdom, the politicians who so rarely seem to understand the implications of their reorganizations and economies, their rationalizations and modernizing, have abolished all the English border regiments. The Durhams are now part of the Light Infantry, an anonymous term which includes such regiments as the Shropshires, the Somersets, and the Duke of Cornwall's. The Northumberland Fusiliers are but another battalion of the Fusiliers, and the Border Regiment has been included in a Lancastrian unit. All these new companions in arms have a mutual respect, and accepted the amalgamations gracefully, if not entirely happily, but whether this is the best possible use of resources is another matter. It may be argued that regiments have never fought better than when they were the 24th or 42nd or 88th, but conditions were very different then and there have been few parts of the army more impressive than the County regiments in two world wars and innumerable other missions.

This book is not, of course, about the border regiments but it naturally makes many references to them, and in some ways explains their fine military records.

Scottish regiments are, very properly, famed throughout the world and have many would-be imitators. Regiments such as the Black Watch, the Greys, the Seaforths, the Gordons, and the Argylls, to name but a few, have fought with a distinction which has almost romanticized the bloody and ugly business of war.

In order to understand the battles which are described in detail later in this book, it is necessary to have a grasp of the main stages in the evolution of Scotland. It will be noted, perhaps with surprise, that Northumberland and Cumberland were once considered part of Scotland. Scottish history is only explicable by reference to earlier history and to geography. It is, unfortunately, not possible to identify many of the very early battlefields precisely, but the visitor who studies the campaigns and the country carefully will probably not be far wrong in his guess. Scotland is very much aware of her past, and rightly proud of the men who made it. We begin therefore by summarizing the main events and drawing attention to matters we feel were of lasting significance.

The fighting qualities of the Scots were noted even in Roman times. Then they were known as Caledonians or Picts and they fought lightly armed and half-naked. Nevertheless they were a formidable threat to the well-equipped, trained, and disciplined Roman legions. Whether they acquired their name because they were *picti* (painted) or whether they were recognized as a branch of the Pictones, a tribe which the Romans had encountered in what is now Portugal, is not known, and never will be. Like many primitive warriors they painted themselves, partly to inspire fear and partly for camouflage; the Romans themselves sometimes did the same. When the Roman general, Agricola, pushed into Scotland in the year 80 he lost many men. But his campaign was meant to intimidate, so he devastated the country up to the Tweed. The next year he pushed further ahead and secured his victories by building a chain of forts between the Forth and the Clyde. Difficult though his progress had been before, it was now noticeably harder. In the year 83 he was campaigning up the east coast. Here he was coming to the heartland of the Caledonians. It would be pleasurable to walk over the battlefield where he fought with them at 'Mons Graupius' but our knowledge of that battle is so limited that we do not even know precisely where it was fought. It is generally believed that it was in the region just to the south-west of Aberdeen. However we do at least possess Tacitus's book, *Agricola*. Agricola was Tacitus's father-in-law and was at the time Governor of Britain, which was classed as a Roman province. Tacitus describes the campaign as follows:

Sending on his fleet therefore to excite a wide and indefinite alarm by devastating several places, and with a light-armed force in which he had incorporated the most valiant of the Britons, and such as were tested by long fidelity he arrived at the Grampian hills, which the enemy had already invested. For the Britons [by which he means the Caledonians] never dispirited

15

by the result of the late engagement, and anticipating vengeance or slavery, and taught at length that their common danger could be fended off by unanimity alone, had called into action the powers of all the states by embassies and confederacies. More than thirty thousand armed men were now available, and still all the youths were pouring in, and even those whose age was fresh and vigorous, distinguished in the field, and bearing their several trophies. On this occasion a chieftain, named Galgacus, eminent among the rest in valour and rank, is said to have addressed the assembled throng, clamouring for battle, to the following effect:

'We have no territory behind us, nor is even the sea secure while the Roman fleet hovers round us so that resistance and war, creditable to the brave, are also safest. The late engagements in which we strove with alternating success against the Romans depended for hopes and means upon our hands, because we, the noblest nation of all Britain, and therefore dwelling in its deepest recesses, and not even beholding the shores of bondsmen, have kept our eyes untainted by the infection of tyranny. Dwelling upon the utmost limits of the earth and freedom, our very remoteness, the last retreat of heroism, has hitherto defended us. Now the extremity of Britain is exposed and the unknown is ever indefinitely grand. There is now no nation beyond us, nothing save the billows and the rocks and the Romans, still more savage, whose tyranny you will in vain appease by submission and concession. Alone of all men they covet with equal rapacity the rich and the needy. Plunder, murder and robbery, under false pretences, they call "Empire" and when they make a wilderness they call it "Peace".'

This dramatic speech is highly revealing. Not only does it give numbers – and here we may trust them – but it also throws considerable light on the mental attitude of the ancient inhabitants of Scotland. The same attitude persisted in many later centuries. It showed an intense passion for freedom and independence, and an equally strong desire not to be conquered by the Romans whom they considered to be less civilized than themselves. Galgacus is apparently well informed about what went on in areas the Romans had already subdued:

> Our wives and sisters, though they escape forcible violation, are insulted under pretexts of friendship and hospitality. Our possessions and properties they consume in taxes, our crops in subsidies. They wear out our bodies and strength in stripes and degradation, in clearing roads through fens and forests. . . . Abandoning all help of indulgence therefore take courage at last, as well those who value their safety as they to whom glory is most dear. Do you believe that the same value is present in the Romans on the battlefield as is proportionate to their insolence in peace . . . they have nothing formidable to fall back on – empty fortresses, colonies of old men, borough-towns disaffected between refractory subjects and tyrannical governors. On the one side you have a general and an army; on the other the taxes, the mines and all the penalties of slavery; and to perpetuate these for ever, or to avenge them, now awaits decision on this plain. Therefore as you march to action, remember your ancestors – think of posterity.

This speech, somewhat abbreviated here, was received with great enthusiasm. Agricola therefore decided to add a few words to his own troops whose morale was high but perhaps not quite high enough. Tacitus mentions that they were with difficulty restrained within the trenches or fortifications. This suggests that when they observed the size of the opposing force they had hastily dug themselves in. Agricola's message does not really concern us for we are not commenting on the Roman martial spirit. His speech was steadier than that of Galgacus but not less inflammatory.

> While Agricola yet spoke, [continues Tacitus] the enthusiasm of the soldiers began to show itself, and a strong excitement followed the conclusion of his address, and they flew at once to

17

arms. In this ardour and impetuosity he so arranged them that the infantry auxiliaries, amounting to eight thousand, formed a strong centre and three thousand cavalry were dispersed on the wings. The legions took their position outside the entrenchments – an arrangement which would be a remarkable distinction to the victory if they succeeded without loss to the Romans – and a resource if they retreated. The lines of the Britons had so taken their stand upon the rising ground – for show and intimidation – that the van formed upon the plain, and the rest, in close array, rose in a manner line above line on the acclivity and the charioteers and cavalry, with cries and evolutions, occupied the intervening space.

It must have been a considerable strain to the nerves to wait through the preliminaries of a battle in those times. Having seen the opposing force and noticed that they outnumbered yours, or were better armed, you then had to listen to a long harangue designed to make you fight to the death and neither give nor ask quarter. It was a foretaste of the atrocity stories of which we should hear so much in later wars, and which would all usually be true in spite of efforts to discredit them.

The Scots (Britons or Caledonians) occupied the period before battle in the most extraordinary evolutions and manoeuvres. The Romans had already noted that they were able to run along their long chariot-poles while their horses were at full gallop and also to leap on and off the chariots while they were hurtling along at speed. Doubtless they dismissed these antics as mere conjuring tricks designed to impress one's own side as much as to intimidate the enemy.

Then Agricola, as the enemy were superior in numbers, apprehending a charge in front and on the flanks, expanded his ranks and, though his lines would apparently be too far extended and many recommended that the legions should be brought up, feeling more sanguine in hope and undismayed by difficulties, he sent back his horse and placed himself on foot before the standards.

At the commencement of the action the contest was maintained from a distance. The Britons, with long swords and narrow shields, firmly and dexterously parried and repelled the missiles of our troops, while they showered upon them a dense volley of their own; until Agricola called upon three cohorts of Batavians and two of the Tungri, to bring the encounter to the sword and closing fight, which was familiar to them from their experience of the service and inconvenient to the enemy, who carried small shields and unwieldy swords. For the swords of the Britons, being unpointed, admitted of no collision or hand-to-hand encounter. Then the Batavians began to repeat their blows, to wound them with the bosses of their shields, to cut their faces, and drive back up the hill those who had opposed them on level ground. The other cohorts, joining in the attack through rivalry or enthusiasm, cut down all who met them, and through their anxiety for victory many were left fainting and unharmed. The troops of enemy cavalry now took to flight and the charioteers entangled themselves among the fighting infantry; though they had spread alarm not yet abated they were impeded by the close ranks of the enemy and the unevenness of the ground. Thus this part of the battle bore no resemblance to a cavalry engagement: after a long and inconvenient wait they were carried along with their horses, and frequently with unmanned chariots and riderless horses, and ran down all who stood in their panic-stricken path.

This account, which is translated fairly literally from the original Latin, at times seems stilted. Nevertheless, it gives a vivid picture of the chaos, confusion, and variety of the battle between Roman legions and Scots. Even a partisan Roman writer cannot obscure the fact that the wild tribesmen of the north had a steadiness and cohesion which more civilized nations might have envied. This becomes increasingly clear as the description continues.

And now the Britons, who had yet taken no part in the action and were posted on the hilltops looking with disdain at our unequal numbers, began to descend and enclose the rear of the Romans, and would have succeeded had not Agricola, apprehending this manoeuvre, opposed their progress with four battalions of cavalry, reserved for emergencies; the more spiritedly they came on the more actively did he disperse them and put them to rout.

What now began to happen was that as the Scots folded themselves around the Roman rear so they themselves were encircled by the Roman reserve cavalry.

Then, [says Tacitus], a strange and awful scene presented itself on the plain. They pursued, they wounded, made prisoners and these, when others came, they put to death. In one place companies of armed men would flee before smaller numbers while others, unarmed, would voluntarily charge forward and rush to their deaths. Arms, bodies and mangled limbs lay everywhere and the ground ran blood. Sometimes, too, fury and courage inspired even the vanquished and when they approached the woods they rallied and cut off the nearest of their pursuers, who were unprepared and did not know the ground.

This was where Agricola's experience and generalship were of paramount importance. He moved rapidly from one part of the field to another and quickly sized up the dangers of the situation. Realizing that he could lose many men in the pursuit, and might even be counterattacked, he hastily posted cohorts along the perimeter of the battlefield. Where there were undergrowth and thickets he strengthened the line with dismounted cavalry. At the same time he despatched other, still mounted, cavalry, to scour the open parts of the woods and to harry the retreating Scots without themselves being ambushed. The organized and methodical pursuit upset the orderly Scottish retreat and men now broke away from their companies and took to flight. Only darkness put an end to the pursuit. Tacitus claims that ten thousand Scots were killed for the loss of only three hundred and sixty Romans but he mentions that among them was a senior commander, high in rank though young in years. The figure of ten thousand for the Scots seems suspiciously high. However, when we consider that the Scots were surrounded on one part of the battlefield, where they were presumably methodically slaughtered, and also put in a fighting withdrawal, their losses were probably in thousands. The Romans had won a day's battle but not a campaign, and for all they knew further resistance might already be assembling. They did not seem to be in entire control of the battlefield, for it is related that the Scots were collecting their wounded, and even trying to release prisoners. Agricola sent out reconnaissance parties the next day but they encountered no further resistance; 'the silence of desolation' was all around.

However, there was no chance of consolidating this victory, for winter was fast approaching. Winter meant withdrawal to 'winter quarters'. No one but a madman would try to campaign during the season of bad weather, particularly in Scotland.

It is a pity that the exact site of Mons Graupius is not known – although some say it is the Hill of Moncrieff. Much may be learned from a battlefield. If we knew the exact site we could work out the tactical plan: where Agricola stationed his reserve, how far away were the hills from which the Scots reserve watched the battle. There is mention of thickets and, to judge by the way the Romans encircled the Scots, thereby turning the tables and effecting a complete tactical surprise, it seems highly likely that the Scots used them for concealment. It should not be impossible to locate sites on which the battle as described by Tacitus could have been fought; and one might be so obvious that it would make the course of the battle perfectly understandable.

Mons Graupius, although the largest, was only one of a series of desperate battles the Scots fought with the Romans. Tactically, Mons Graupius was a mistake and the Scots did not repeat it. In future they did not oppose the Romans in solid formations which the Romans could attack in their own way and in their own time; instead they resorted to raids and to luring the Romans into ambushes whenever possible. The Romans had had too much experience of this type of warfare to be caught often, and, instead of being drawn into wasteful fights in the heart of rugged Scotland, they decided to bar the Scots out of territories they themselves controlled. There were no more combined operations of the kind favoured by Agricola with the fleet sailing round the coast while the army probed inland. Instead, the Emperor Hadrian visited Britain in the year 120 and ordered that a wall should be built from the Tyne to the Solway. In its declining years the Roman Empire resorted to this expedient for keeping out what they called 'the barbarians'. Vast walls were built around whole countries, even though history had already proved the futility of such enterprise. 'If you wish for peace, prepare for war', and 'attack is the best form of defence' were well-known Roman slogans, but they did not always put them into practice. Hadrian's Wall, which took eighteen years to build and was strengthened by forts and towers at intervals, extended over seventy miles. It is an impressive monument today but was apparently less so to the Picts and Scots, for they attacked it incessantly and climbed over it apparently at will. As soon as two years after it had been built, the policy on which it was planned was abandoned and the Romans decided that it was necessary to push farther north. This brought to fame a Roman general named Lollius Urbicus, of whom little is known; but his achievements are a memorial of no mean kind. He drove the marauding Scots back to the line between the Forth and Clyde and then carried out the command of the Emperor Antoninus Pius to build yet another wall to hold them there. Unfortunately for Rome, the Antonine line proved to be no more impassable than Hadrian's Wall. Both are, however, a tribute to the Roman skill in military engineering, and are a joy to twentieth-century visitors; neither achieved its original purpose which was to keep out the northern raiders.

Our only source of information for the events of what might be called the early Dark Ages is Roman. In the year 200, the walls were clearly failing to control the border, for we have ominous reports of two tribes known respectively as the Caledonians and the Maeatae. So great was their menace that the Emperor Severus himself decided to deal with it, and in 208 he set off at the head of a punitive expedition. Like many a great general after him, he had to travel in a litter (he was elderly and much troubled by gout) and, like some of his successors, he was remarkably unsuccessful. But the Scots were not forgetful of the lesson they had learnt nearly 150 years before; instead of giving battle where it would have suited the Romans they led them on and on, frequently ambushing them but often merely melting away and letting climate and terrain do the rest. It is said, though doubtless with exaggeration, that Severus lost 50,000 men in this so-called punitive expedition. He was said to have reached 'the extremity of the island' whatever that may have meant. However, he seems to have had some success, for he extracted a treaty from the Caledonians by which they renounced their claim to some disputed territory. He is also credited with having built the 'Severus' wall but no one knows where it was meant to be, for no trace of it can be found.

Severus was, however, a fighter, pressing on, undeterred by losses and respected by his adversaries. His death in 211, when he was apparently planning another expedition, marks the end of formal Roman attempts to subdue Scotland. One hundred years later a brave attempt was made to intimidate the Scots when Theodosius was despatched to the border by the Roman Emperor, Valentinian. Valentinian was a soldier of no mean order and, although the Empire he represented was crumbling, the Picts and Scots could not have been aware of it. Instead he drove them back with a series of vigorous attacks, isolating and cutting them off with a tactical skill which earned more than one victory. In respect for his achievement they ceded an unknown area which was called Valentia.

But it could not last; Rome was in decline. To their credit the Romans still tried to hold the boundaries of their Empire, but soon Rome itself was threatened and they had to withdraw. Perhaps their most durable monument, apart from Hadrian's Wall and the Antonine Wall, was Ptolemy's Geography. Although Ptolemy lived in Alexandria, Scotland appears in his atlas which lists seventeen tribes and nineteen towns. Some of this may be intelligent guesswork, or even mere hearsay, but much of it is probably well founded. You cannot fight a people for hundreds of years and sign treaties with them without acquiring some knowledge of their territories and resources. And if the Romans learnt something from the Scots, the Scots too must have learnt something from the invaders; not least was the need to combine, and yet, while combining, to fulfil a guerrilla role. It would not be an exaggeration to say that the Romans gave the first impetus to the unity of Scotland. Indirectly they initiated the tremendous religious fervour which has often spurred on Scottish armies. St Ninian, of whom very little is known, appears to have been the first missionary who tried to convert the Scots to Christianity. This was in the late fourth century and we do not know how much success he had in his lifetime, although he is said to have founded a church in Galloway. Even if the Romans had been able to stay in Britain and support him his task would have been formidable enough but as the Roman legions were all withdrawn during the early years of the next century it is hardly surprising that his achievements lacked permanence.

Saints in those days were not to be trifled with. A king who opposed St Ninian went blind. St Ninian restored his sight and enlisted him as a supporter. After St Ninian's death his relics cured the sick and terrified the wicked. Sixty churches were dedicated to him. However, his earthly achievements were as nothing to those of St Mungo of Strathclyde. When a hostile king mocked him for his poverty, a timely storm flooded the Clyde and swept away the royal granaries; fortuitously they were stranded just by the saint's house. Much displeased, the king and his chief minister rode off to punish St Mungo, and kicked him. The chief minister was then thrown from his horse and broke his neck; the king's foot swelled and caused his death; all his family then died one by one of the same affliction of the feet!

In the sixth century we find four different groups struggling for the mastery of Scotland. These were the Picts, the Britons, the Angles, and the Scots.

The Picts commanded the largest stretch of territory, for they were supreme in the whole area north of the Forth. At certain periods they divided into two groups, the northern and the southern, but most of the time were under one king who had minor kings under him. The Picts were Celts.

In the south-west, in the Strathclyde area, were Britons. These were the same stock as the inhabitants of Britain who had first opposed the Romans in 55 B.C. Four hundred years of Roman occupation had softened them, and after the Romans withdrew they were unable to defend themselves against the Saxons. Some settled in Cornwall, some in Wales, and some reached southern Scotland. Once in Scotland they had no choice but to recover some of their former warrior spirit. For centuries they were constantly under attack from north, east, and south. Not surprisingly, the inhabitants of that area in later years acquired a reputation for dour, tenacious military stamina.

On the west, in what is now Argyllshire (then called the Kingdom of Dalriada), was a colony of Celts who had come from Ireland. These, curiously enough, were known as the Scots. They contrived to maintain links with Ireland and also to avoid being absorbed by the northern Picts.

In addition there were the Angles. Some time during the sixth century, the Angles, who eventually gave their name to England, settled in the area just south of the Firth of Forth. This was called Bernicia and soon included the place which is now Edinburgh, as well as the fortress of Bamburgh in Northumbria.

Further to these there were three minor groupings which, though small, would play an important part in the future. These were Calatria, Mannan (note Clackmannan), and Galloway. The former two were eventually absorbed, but the inhabitants of Galloway were more enduring. Domiciled in the area now covered by Wigton and Kirkcudbright, it seemed at one stage that they, not the Picts, might dominate Scotland.

At the end of the sixth century, two hundred years after St Ninian had made his missionary attempt, the Picts were converted to Christianity by St Columba. Some part of Columba's success was due to the fact that he was a Christian soldier; when he laid aside the Bible for the broadsword, he earned respect from all sides. Among his other martial feats are said to be the slaying of a Loch Ness monster! Christianity, even if somewhat militant, caused national unity to become one step nearer, but it did not, of course, signify the end of battles, for war was a recreation and a way of life. During different periods, power ebbed and flowed from one area to another, but in the seventh and eighth centuries it is clear that a main area of hostility was building up along what we now describe as the border country. The activities of minor kings and chiefs on unknown battlefields are of significance to us only so far as they helped form a military pattern. Scotland was being born with all its remarkable regional characteristics. In the ninth century, Kenneth MacAlpin did much for the future kingdom of Scotland by transferring the seat of government from Iona to Dunkeld. Here the bones of St Columba were reinterred, making it a religious shrine as well as a political and military headquarters. But now, Scotland, like England, was attacked by more and more formidable foes. With Danes on one side and Norwegians on the other, it seemed that all that precarious Scottish unity and identity might be swept away. The Norwegians occupied the Orkneys and most of Caithness and Sutherland. The chronicle of battle, murder, and sudden death does not concern us here; suffice it to say that only at the beginning of the eleventh century did Scotland begin to assume her final form. Even so it would be the thirteenth century before the Scottish crown symbolized a physical Kingdom rather than a concept. Curiously enough, in the early part of this period, Scotland had to absorb refugees from Norman England; for, after the Battle of Hastings and the 'harrying of the north', many English wished for nothing better than to put themselves well out of reach of Norman law, taxation and tyranny.

Early in the eleventh century Scotland as we now know it began to take shape. Malcolm II, who reigned from 1005 to 1034, was largely responsible.* Malcolm gained Lothian and soon

---

* Scotland at this time was known as Alba.

added Strathclyde to it. When Malcolm died he was succeeded by his grandson, Duncan. Duncan, who reigned for six years, has acquired an impressive reputation through being favourably represented in Shakespeare's *Macbeth*:

> *this Duncan*
> *Hath born his faculties so meek, hath been*
> *So clear in his great office.*

In fact, his six-year reign was one of almost unbroken disaster. His courage was not in question but his military skill did not match it. Every army he contrived to raise was scattered by his opponents and his fleet was no luckier. Macbeth, whose own claim to the throne was as good as Duncan's, eventually led a rebellion against this unhappy king and killed him at Bothgouanan, near Elgin. Macbeth's own reign between 1040 and 1057 was militarily successful. Furthermore he was an enthusiastic supporter of the church and distributed alms liberally. He was even said to have made a pilgrimage to Rome and distributed alms to the poor there. He was eventually killed in battle at Lumphanan in Aberdeenshire, not at Dunsinane where he fought an inconclusive battle. In view of this it might be wondered why Shakespeare depicted him as a treacherous villain and an unsuccessful one as well. The answer is that Shakespeare took his character from Holinshed, who in turn took his Macbeth from Wyntoun. Wyntoun was anxious to prove that the Scottish royal line stretched unbroken back to the dawn of history. As Macbeth was not of the direct line he had to be classed as a villainous usurper who had temporarily and illegally worn the crown.

Macbeth's successor was Malcolm III also known as Malcolm Canmore. The distinguished name, 'Canmore' literally means 'big head' and is typical of the day when a man's name came from a physical deformity, his habits, or his job. Thus the Stuart was a sty-ward or pig-keeper; Ponsford meant 'fat guts'; Bevin meant 'drinker'; and Cruikshanks described almost anyone with a limp. However, big head or not, Malcolm had a successful thirty-six year reign. Not only did he maintain a stable régime in Scotland;

he also pushed his area of influence down to the Tyne. After one of his raids it was said that every cottage in Scotland had an English slave working in it. However, when William the Conqueror took an army and a fleet to Scotland Malcolm signed a treaty without fighting. It was, nevertheless, improbable that peace between Scotland and England could last, and we find that, when William went to France in 1079, the opportunity his absence presented to Malcolm was irresistible. Once again the Tweed–Tyne area was devastated. Once again, when the English took a great army to Scotland, it found no army to fight, nor supplies to live on, and eventually withdrew hoping that the threat had been enough; needless to say it had not. A somewhat better anti-invasion precaution was to build castles along the border route. One of them was New Castle on the Tyne.

In 1091 in the reign of William II (Rufus) Malcolm decided that the English would be fair game again, especially since Rufus was in Normandy, having considerable trouble with his brother Robert. On this occasion Malcolm miscalculated, for his forces were held and then forced to withdraw. Subsequently, Rufus came north with a large army and fleet. The fleet was wrecked in a storm, but the army invaded Lothian. Yet again there was no pitched battle, but Rufus annexed Carlisle and what is now Cumberland. This at the time was southern Strathclyde, the refuge of the Britons from Wales; it has been an English county ever since. Malcolm was prepared to give feudal homage to the English crown, but the annexation of part of Strathclyde was more than he could stomach. He travelled to Gloucester to protest in person to Rufus, but the English King refused even to see him. Once again Malcolm set out to harry the English border. Although his wife Margaret begged him not to go, he insisted on leading the expedition and ran into an ambush at Alnwick. It seems that some of his chiefs were not entirely reliable. Malcolm was killed, and, without his controlling hand, the army fell apart. Retreating hastily into Scotland, the Scots lost many men in trying to cross rivers which were swollen by rains; it was an unrelieved disaster. Malcolm's body was taken to Tynemouth in a peasant's cart. It was 1093. Seven years later William Rufus would be killed by an arrow while hunting in the New Forest and he too would make his last journey in a peasant's cart.

'Behind every great man stands a great woman.' In this case it was Queen Margaret. She was English by birth, being a granddaughter of Edward the Confessor, and did something to alleviate the miseries of those taken prisoner by her husband. She also established some refinements in the Scottish court and apparently took a leading part in administration when her husband was away. Her most noticeable characteristic was her piety, which went as far as self-mortification. As well as practising ascetic self-denial, she completed a routine of unattractive tasks, such as washing the feet of the poor and dressing offensive sores. She even made Malcolm take part in some of these ceremonies. When she died, four days after her husband, it was indeed a moment of truth; there was widespread reaction against the power she had wielded. Malcolm's brother tried to seize the throne in place of her sons and, to destroy a legend, to capture her body from Edinburgh Castle where it was still lying. Margaret's sons carried it away in secret but then had to flee themselves. The next few years saw brief reigns and intermittent bloodshed; then Scotland became more settled. In the twelfth century we find the notorious Alexander I, 'the Fierce', who married Sibylla, one of the illegitimate daughters of Henry I of England.* Henry I, incidentally, founded Norham Castle on the Tweed to help 'keep the border'; few castles have seen as much fighting as Norham. Alexander established the monastery of Scone, which he peopled with Augustinian monks from Yorkshire. On the charters from his reign appear names – among them were Bruce, Lindsay, Umphraville and FitzAlan – which were to recur over and over again in Scottish history. In spite of his nickname, acquired when suppressing some of his dissident subjects, Alexander was genuinely religious. When he died in 1124, his brother David, who succeeded him,

---

* Henry I's wife was even more devout and ascetic than Queen Margaret of Scotland had been but Henry, the man who was said never to have smiled for fifteen years, had a distinct proclivity for begetting 'natural' offspring.

was no less competent though less independent. David had the backing of those Norman knights who had settled in Scotland. He was therefore able to consolidate his kingdom and even to extend it slightly. However, co-operation with the English throne led him into considerable difficulties when the English crown was disputed between Matilda, daughter of Henry I, and Stephen, his nephew. As Matilda was David's niece he was bound to support her. His support took a very practical turn in 1136 when he took an army across the border and captured every castle in Cumberland and Northumberland with the exception of Bamburgh. Stephen, always ready for another long gruelling campaign, however strategically unwise, set off north to teach him a lesson. The lesson, in the event, was not needed, for David, recognizing a fellow warrior, promptly signed a treaty by which he agreed to give no further trouble.

Treaties, of course, are only durable if they are made in good faith and are enforceable. This one was neither. On the strength of an insult to his son, David decided that England must be taught a lesson once more; he therefore set off southwards, destroying and burning. It was said that he tried to restrain the wilder atrocities but was apparently largely unsuccessful. Stephen came up to meet him, and David then retreated skilfully. Near Roxburgh, the Scottish king laid a most ingenious ambush. Whether Stephen learnt of this through spies, or whether he had a nose for a dangerous situation, is not on record, but the result was that he slipped by, devastated the surrounding countryside, and returned south without loss. This manoeuvre was not entirely to Stephen's liking, for he enjoyed a battle as a modern man enjoys a football match, but the news from England was so ominous that he dared not stay away longer.

It now seemed to David that the north of England was his for the taking, and that afterwards he need only march to join up with his niece, Matilda. With suitable piety he waited till the end of Lent before beginning his invasion and then drove south like a Scottish Jenghiz Khan. He captured Norham castle and besieged Wark: the former strength of Wark is unfortunately not easily observable today but the fact that he made it impotent was in itself a terrifying threat. At the same time another Scottish army, under William Fitz-Duncan, was driving down to Clitheroe, where it swept away a hastily-assembled English force. This was a useful diversion and good for morale but not really relevant to the main push. David therefore called Fitz-Duncan's men back, and united them with his own force. His scouts informed him that a considerable English army was mustering on his route to York. But, if and when he captured York, the way to the south would be open. His army was now said to number as many as 26,000 – unlikely but just possible.

The situation was a little more complicated than it appears on the surface. Seemingly, David of Scotland was marching south to overwhelm the forces of the English king. Faced with this challenge, all the knights of the north would rally to repel the invader who had come to ravage their lands and enslave them. To some extent this is what happened, for Thurstan, Archbishop of York, a man of great age and venerability, mustered a large army whose members were encouraged to believe they were fighting a holy war. As a symbol of their divine commission they carried a ship's mast draped with four cathedral banners; at the top was a pyx enclosing a sacred wafer. But as a result of the Normanization of Scotland some of the English barons held nearly as much land over the border as they held in England and through this they owed allegiance to David because he was King of Scotland. Two of them, whose names are more renowned in Scottish than in English history, were Robert de Bruce and Bernard de Balliol. The pair galloped forward to David's camp and pledged that if he now retired his son would be made Earl of Northumberland. David rejected the offer. But, if the English army contained men with dual allegiance, the Scottish included even more divisive elements. Some were Norwegians from the Orkneys, others were Angles who had settled in Lothian; yet others were Normans, and with them were apparently German mercenaries. But the most separated of all were the men of Galloway, whose appearance well displayed their savage ferocity. They were poorly armed and

31

almost naked, circumstances which did not prevent their insisting on their traditional right to be the van of the Scottish army. In that position they received the full shock of the English archers. These, though not possessing the length and accuracy of the long-bowmen who would create such devastation in later battles, were more than a match for the unarmoured Galwegians, who were cut down at thirty yards' range. David himself was stationed behind them and, without being able to affect the issue, saw the Galwegian leader killed and the whole contingent plunged into confusion. On the right, Prince Henry of Scotland, the aspirant to the Earldom of Northumberland, commanded a wing of Norman knights and Norwegian auxiliaries, which proved all too effective. Having borne away the English left, it pursued it into wet and soggy ground, but there they were caught by the English centre which had regrouped after its easy victory over the Galwegians. Prince Henry escaped from the trap he had created for his force but only at the expense of one hundred and eighty knights of his two-hundred-strong bodyguard.

This bloody clash, at Northallerton, went into history as 'The Battle of the Standard'. It could have been decisive had the dis-organized Scottish army been harried and pursued back into its own lands. But Stephen was too preoccupied with his own civil war to be able to consolidate this unexpected victory. Instead, David was able to besiege and capture Wark castle, which had previously defied all his efforts to take it. A year later a truce was signed between David and Stephen in which David's son was granted the Earldom of Northumberland on condition that he assisted Stephen against Matilda (who was his cousin). To make good the promise, Henry now took up residence in England and Stephen was confirmed in his possession of the castles of Bamburgh and Newcastle. David was in no way inhibited by this solemn undertaking and two years later was fighting for Matilda at Winchester; he was lucky not to be taken prisoner in the dramatic siege of the castle. The situation then, and during the next eight years is bizarre in the extreme. Treachery seems to have been the rule rather than the exception. Contestants changed sides with almost frivolous alacrity, and Henry's allegiance to Stephen proved to be of short duration. At this time David and his Scottish followers were firmly convinced that Carlisle and Newcastle were the true frontier towns of Scotland. This belief long persisted.

David however had his own internal troubles which throw some light on the uncertainties of kingship at this time. A renegade monk – from Lancashire – named Wimund, suddenly claimed to be Earl of Moray and raised a considerable and formidable force from the Western Isles. He proved to be unbeatable in that he could never be cornered in a battle; the only solution was to buy him off. Even that proved unsatisfactory, and Wimund ceased to trouble David only when a number of his own men, tired of his greed and irascibility, blinded him and confined him in a Yorkshire monastery. After all these troubles David might have looked forward with some confidence to a peaceful old age. But it was not to be. His son and heir, Henry, died young, and David had to go to enormous trouble to enforce the claims of his grandchildren. However, on balance, the verdict of history is that David exerted a positive influence for good. Church and state power both increased during his reign, although the method by which this was effected was not to everyone's liking. Normans, Saxons and Danes were encouraged to settle in Scotland. Fitzalans and Morevilles now begin to appear as Scottish landowners. Even more significant was the introduction of Norman law, Norman custom, and even Norman trade. The Normans were already in the Mediterranean and their discoveries such as rice, figs, almonds pepper, and ginger were articles of commerce wherever the Norman tentacles penetrated, and Scotland was no exception. Whatever David's faults and mistakes, his contribution to Scotland's unity was considerable. The need for a strong king was all too apparent when his twelve-year-old grandson, Malcolm IV, succeeded him. Much of the ensuing trouble came from the house of Moray, and, when this was settled, Malcolm found himself getting the worst of hard bargaining over the border counties with Henry II of England. At the age of sixteen Malcolm was deeply

33

affronted by Henry II's refusal to dub him a knight. However, even a king had to 'win his spurs', and it took a year's service in France in the English army before Malcolm gained that coveted honour. In view of the disturbed state of Scotland in his absence the knighthood was hard won; when Malcolm died at the early age of twenty-four the crown went to his brother William.

William, known as 'the Lion', reigned a surprisingly long time – forty-nine years – but his reign was not without its setbacks. He had the optimistic ambition of extending Scottish territory by adding in Northumberland and Cumberland; it was not an aspiration likely to find favour with a king like Henry II of England. But in 1173 he set off to translate ambition into fact. Aided by the men of Galloway, whose purposeless savagery was enough to drive the most passive opposition to heights of frenzied resistance, he invaded Northumberland. Then, somewhat erratically, he veered west and besieged Carlisle. By 1174 he was back at Alnwick where, injudiciously, he allowed himself to be separated from the main part of his army. In the morning mist, he was surprised by a party of English knights who promptly took him prisoner. He was sent south to Northampton castle and from there transferred to even safer custody at Falaise, the birthplace of William the Conqueror. The price of his freedom was the acknowledgement of Henry II as his feudal superior, the installation of English garrisons at Berwick, Edinburgh, Jedburgh, Roxburgh, and Stirling castles, and the acceptance of English jurisdiction over the Scottish church. This, the Treaty of Falaise of 1176, was a bitter pill to swallow but it remained in force for fifteen years.

William's absence and subsequent subjection to a humiliating treaty led to predictable disturbances in his own kingdom. Galloway became virtually independent and the north was no better. Not least of William's troubles was that he had to request permission from Henry II to take up arms against rebels in his own territories.

On Henry II's death in 1189 the situation brightened notably for William. Richard I, Coeur de Lion, showed little interest in his English throne and during his ten-year reign spent only eight months in England. His ambition was to capture Jerusalem and his main interests were fighting in France or other overseas territories. He accomplished a neat stroke of business by selling back to the Scots their independence for 10,000 marks, thereby financing his next expedition and also gaining Scottish goodwill and friendship in the process. However, he did not relinquish Northumberland and Cumberland, which at that time were still thought to be Scottish by right if not by law.

In 1199 Richard I was dead and his place had been taken by his evasive brother, John, who, although a capable warrior when he bestirred himself, was not a man anyone could respect or trust. William's efforts to strike a bargain over the disputed counties led to nothing but frustration, and soon it seemed as though the two countries would be at war again. In 1204 John was trying to build a fortress at the mouth of the Tweed to dominate the town of Berwick, but every move he made to do so was frustrated by the Scots. Eventually, in 1209, John decided that the Scots must be taught a lesson and the fortress must be built. He assembled a huge army and marched north. William took up station at Roxburgh and it seemed as if a massive blood-bath was now inevitable. But, curiously enough, this was merely a show of force and neither king really wanted a fight to the death. In consequence, emissaries from either side negotiated a treaty. It was a simple enough arrangement: John agreed not to build his proposed castle at Tweedmouth and William agreed to pay 15,000 marks for any injuries John had suffered. The gainer was probably William who had everything to lose from an exhausting battle in the border country; even if he won it his army would be so weakened that the rebels in his kingdom would become uncontrollable. As it was, Caithness was within a hair's breadth of becoming an independent kingdom. It had produced intractable warriors with names like Sigurd the Stout and Thorfin the Ugly, and now had Guthred, who in 1211 looked like being the greatest menace of all. More by luck than skill William precariously hung on.

Limited though his achievements were, William probably deserved the title 'the Lion'. His setbacks might have ruined a lesser man. Kings have reigned for longer but few have seen such incessant action. When he died in 1214 Scotland was in no worse state than when he had inherited. This might seem a slight achievement for a fifty-year reign but it must not be forgotten that few kings have had to contend so long against so many discordant elements in his kingdom. And a man's work may often be judged by its aftermath; in this case the aftermath was Scotland's 'golden age'.

Like William, his successor, Alexander II, came to the throne young, indeed, he was only sixteen. Within a year he – or rather, his lieutenant, the Earl of Ross – had crushed the inevitable rebellion in Moray. Unwisely – perhaps because he listened to bad advice – Alexander allied himself to the English barons who were banding together against King John. His next move was to take an army over the border to besiege Norham Castle. He and his advisers had underrated the military ability of John, which, though it functioned only spasmodically, was in no way inferior to that of his father, Henry II or his brother, the more renowned Richard I. John's army came storming north; the bulk of it composed of mercenaries whom he could trust as long as his purse lasted – which was longer than some of his feudal subjects. Alexander withdrew to the Esk and then waited, prepared to give battle for Edinburgh. But it began to look as if by mutual consent a boundary between England and Scotland would eventually be agreed. It would become a 'march' – a frontier area where lands would be held by powerful barons, later to be known as 'marcher lords', who would be equally ready for an aggressive or a defensive battle, and to relish one as much as the other. They built and held great castles and feared no one; the only admiration they coveted was that of their traditional foes. Such men might not contribute much to the social life of the country in which they lived but they had a stabilizing effect on frontiers.

In 1216 King John of England died and was succeeded by Henry III, then a boy of only nine. His throne, in a country seething with turbulent barons, looked anything but secure, but eventually he had one of the longest reigns in English history –

fifty-six years. Even more surprising is the fact that he retained it – except for one year – in spite of crass stupidity and exasperating folly. Equally, the first five years of Alexander's reign gave little promise of a bright future; but in 1221 he married Henry's sister. At the same time he married off his own sister to Hubert de Burgh, the Great Justiciar, who was the wisest and most powerful man in England at the time. Stability and peace were thus assured and Alexander's hands were freed to deal with internal problems. The first of these was Argyll, the old Dalriada, which had never been properly subject to the Scottish crown; it had come to the fore only when it had fostered rebellions or supported Scotland's enemies. Strangely enough, when Alexander led an expedition composed of men from Lothian and Galloway into Argyll there was no opposition. He therefore confiscated territory from potential troublemakers and distributed it to those whom he hoped would be his friends. It was a notable step forward but not the end of rebellion and disorder, which were inevitable; but they were no longer inevitably disastrous. An even more significant step was taken in 1237 when, at a conference in York, the frontier between England and Scotland was legally agreed. In return for abandoning his claim to Northumberland and Cumberland Alexander received lands in those counties to the value of £200 a year.

The year 1237 was therefore a vital one in the history of Anglo-Scottish relations. Before that date there had been endless wars and expeditions over a disputed unmarked frontier. After 1237 there were still centuries of battle and bloodshed to come; but it would be warfare of a different kind, in which a man's country would as often as not be more important than his clan or his family.

Five years after the Treaty of York, however, it seemed that the new stability would be shattered suddenly, the cause of which seems trivial to us today. In 1242 a tournament was held at Haddington. Now, tournaments, like football matches today, were meant to act as a safety-valve for violent feelings, to encourage knightly skills, and to provide spectacular entertainment. They seldom failed in the last capacity but, again not unlike the modern football match, were notable more for engendering ill-feeling than for dispelling it. A tournament was a miniature battle between troops of knights using lances; the only unwarlike concession was to point one's lance at an opponent's body and not his head. In between the tournaments there would be jousts, single-handed combats in which the jousters began with lances and continued with axes and swords. Two years before the Haddington incident there had been a tournament at Cologne in which sixty combatants had been killed.

At Haddington, Patrick of Galloway, Earl of Atholl, unhorsed Walter Bisset, a Norman baron from Moray. The same night Atholl's lodging was burnt to the ground and he himself died in the flames. The Atholls and the Bissets already hated each other, and this was clearly a matter which could only be avenged by bloodletting. To avert an internecine fracas which might lead to widespread trouble and disruption, Alexander – under pressure from his barons – agreed that the Bissets should be put on trial. Needless to say they proclaimed their innocence, and were probably telling the truth, but this availed them nothing. Too many people testified against them and as a result Bisset was banished and his estates forfeited.

Bisset promptly went to the English court where he did his utmost to poison relations between England and Scotland. His task was not difficult, for Henry was already suspicious of the close relationship Alexander was establishing with the French. As news of war preparations flew from one side to the other, so the armies grew. Eventually, Alexander took a great army to the frontier of Northumberland. Meanwhile, Henry took as big an army to Newcastle. A clash appeared imminent but, as on former occasions, there were too many people on each side who thought that a major battle would be damaging to their own interests. Messages were exchanged and, as a result, the two kings agreed not to fight. It was dangerous brinkmanship, but the final calamity was averted.

Seven years later Alexander died, succumbing to a mysterious illness while on an expedition to conquer the Sudreys, in the

Western Isles, which still belonged to Norway. He was succeeded by his son, a boy of eight, who became Alexander III. The year was 1249.

Quite unpredictably the new king reigned thirty-seven years during which there was very little formal fighting. Yet, all through his reign, there was a conflict between the pro-English faction, led by Durward, and the Scottish independence group, led by Comyn, Earl of Menteith, whose family included two earls and thirty knights. Initially the Comyn faction was in the ascendant. Then, with English help, the Durwards displaced it. The Comyns, however, were not to be brushed on one side lightly, as will be appreciated from their subsequent history. In 1257 they kidnapped Alexander himself and made him their prisoner in Stirling Castle. Durward fled to England. Henry III of England was furious at this treatment of one whom he had hoped would be his vassal king, but in that year he had too many subversive elements in his own kingdom to risk sending an army into Scotland. Applying what he thought was remarkable subtlety to the solution of the problem, he sent the Earls of Hereford and Albemarle, with John de Balliol (originally Bailleul) to a conference at Jedburgh. The English had a substantial force at Norham, with which it was hoped to achieve a counter-revolution in Scotland; the Comyns, however, had an equally large force hidden in the woods around Jedburgh. As the conference got under way, Scots spearmen appeared silently and surrounded the meeting-place. The result was a compromise in which Scotland became a regency with four Englishmen among the ten members of the Regency Council. The Comyns had triumphed.

Relations between the two countries were not unduly strained despite the wariness of all the principals. While never entirely sure of his position in regard to England, Alexander nevertheless managed to make a substantial and enduring contribution to Scottish unity. In 1262 he sent a message to King Haco of Norway suggesting that the Hebrides might now become part of Scotland by negotiation, but Haco treated the invitation with scorn and, in 1263, set out with a large fleet to reassert his claims and demand fealty in the islands. Initially he was successful, and received widespread homage, but an untimely storm decimated his shipping. After being driven on to the Scottish mainland, he was ferociously attacked by Alexander's supporters. He escaped, but on the way home died from an undefined sickness.

Alexander was quick to take advantage of this military vacuum. First he reassembled an army which he proposed to launch against the King of Man who had given fealty to Haco. It was not necessary. Magnus, King of Man, presented himself to Alexander at Dumfries and swore homage. The Hebrides soon followed suit.

Towards the end of his long reign which had begun so inauspiciously but developed so well, there were ominous signs of trouble ahead. Alexander's children all predeceased him. He was only forty-four and had married again in 1285, but the best hope for Scotland's future lay in the infant daughter of his sister, Margaret, who had married King Eric of Norway after Haco's death. Margaret had died in 1283, and the infant 'Maid of Norway' was the only direct heir to the ancient line of Scotland. When her mother died, she had been acknowledged at the age of one by thirteen earls, eleven bishops, and twenty-five barons as heiress of Scotland, the Hebrides, the Isle of Man, Tynedale, and Penrith.

Two years later, as we saw above, Alexander married again, and the marriage-feast was held in Jedburgh Abbey. As part of the entertainment a pageant was held and included a popular medieval masque known as the Dance of Death, a sombre entertainment which included amongst its *dramatis personae* a rather realistic skeleton. The spectators were uncertain whether this was part of the entertainment or whether a ghostly demoniac figure had intruded; in consequence many predicted that the outlook for the king was baleful indeed. Nor were they to be disappointed; that winter had more than its share of ominous thunderstorms. On 19 March 1286 Alexander held a council in Edinburgh castle. It took all day but, although darkness had fallen on a particularly stormy night, Alexander insisted that he must ride home to the queen at Kinghorn. He crossed the ferry and reached Inverkeithing. It was now so dark that no one could see beyond his horse's head, and, just outside Kinghorn itself, Alexander's horse suddenly stumbled over the cliff, killing its rider.

It was a shock for Scotland but not a calamity. A regency was proclaimed to reign for the young queen, who was still in Norway, and her succession was accepted.

Edward I of England, who had just completed the conquest of Wales in 1286 now saw a golden opportunity to unite England and Scotland. There was, at this time, no real enmity between the two countries; in fact they had much in common and considerable empathy. The battles and border skirmishes of the past were either forgotten or recognized as minor stages in the development of a rational frontier. There was no hint of the bitterness to come, neither in the relationship between England and Scotland nor in the internal politics of Scotland itself.

Edward's idea, eminently sensible, was that the unity of Britain might well be furthered by the marriage of his son, Edward, the new Prince of Wales, to little Margaret, the new queen of Scotland. Edward was careful not to propose to interfere with Scottish law or liberty and made this clear in the agreement he put to the Scottish regents. The regents accepted his good faith, although within months he was suggesting that, to guard against a rumoured rebellion, certain Scottish castles should be put in his hands, a proposal that was firmly refused.

In September 1290 a ship was sent to Norway to bring the seven-year-old queen to her kingdom of Scotland, a country she had never seen.

The details of that appalling journey are not known but it seems that, after an unduly long voyage in which the ship was tossed around by gales, she was landed at Kirkwall, only to die. The story, not surprisingly, passed into Scottish legend as the ballad of Sir Patrick Spens. It begins impressively, even if inaccurately,

*The King sits in Dumfermline town,*
*Drinking the blood-red wine;*
*'O where shall I get a skeely skipper*
*To sail this ship of mine.'*

41

Sir Patrick Spens is nominated and:

> *'To Noroway, to Noroway,*
> *To Noroway, o'er the foam;*
> *The King's daughter of Noroway*
> *'Tis thou must fetch her hame.'*

Sir Patrick was not pleased:

> *'O who is this has done this deed,*
> *Has told the King of me*
> *To send us out at this time of the year,*
> *To sail upon the sea?*
>
> *'Be it wind, be it wet, be it hail, be it sleet,*
> *Our ship must sail the foam*
> *The King's daughter of Noroway*
> *'Tis we must fetch her home.'*

The outward journey was bad enough, but the return was blighted by ill-omen before it even started. And

> *They had not sailed a league, a league,*
> *A league but barely three,*
> *When the lift grew dark and the wind blew loud*
> *And gurly grew the sea.\**
>
> *The ankers brake and the topmasts lap,*
> *It was such a deadly storm;*
> *And the waves came o'er the broken ship*
> *Till all her sides were torn.*

In the ballad, the ship, the crew, and Sir Patrick Spens all finished their voyage 'fifty fathoms deep'. The chronicler records with juicy relish:

---

\* The 'lift' was the sky or air, as in 'aloft'; 'gurly' is untranslatable but perhaps needs no translation.

*'O loth, loth were our good Scots Lords*
*To wet their cork-heel'd shoon,*
*But long ere all the play was play'd*
*They wet their hats aboon*

*And many was the feather-bed*
*That fluttered on the foam;*
*And many was the good lord's son*
*That never more came home.*

The fate of the unfortunate Maid of Norway is overlooked, or perhaps thought a price worth paying, if a fashion-crazy nobility – cork-heeled shoes, indeed – should receive their just deserts. Feather beds as well! What was Scotland coming to?

*'And long, long may the ladies sit*
*With their long combs in their hair,*
*All waiting for their own dear loves*
*For them they'll see no more.*

It is, of course, a sad enough story, of this frail child, motherless and alone, flung around in unprecedented storms on her way to an unknown land, dying perhaps of fear and misery. For Scotland it was even worse, for now there was a disputed succession, carefully watched by an ambitious and dynamic King of England who did not question his right to intervene but was not yet clear about the timing.

In Scotland it appeared as though Bruce of Annandale was the only valid claimant, but this opinion did not commend itself to Edward. He held a conviction, not shared by the Scots, that he was 'Superior and Lord Paramount of Scotland' and should settle the affairs of that country. He announced this at Norham in May 1291 and again in June in an unknown field north of the Tweed. At the second meeting were eight claimants to the Scottish throne; in August the number had increased to twelve, but only three could be seriously considered: John Balliol, Robert Bruce, and Henry Hastings. Hastings was soon eliminated, and on 17 November at Berwick Castle Balliol was proclaimed by Edward the lawful heir to the throne of Scotland. Of the once mighty Berwick castle only earthworks remain and, as with many other castles, railway building has destroyed much of the former precincts. However, Berwick is still a fascinating town, and it may interest the reader to know that, when he stands on the platform of the railway station, he is on the site of the hall where Edward proclaimed Balliol King of Scotland. Technically, Edward's decision was undoubtedly correct, but he must have been as aware as anyone else that the result of appointing a weak character like Balliol could result in nothing but disaster for Scotland, however satisfactory it might be for English suzerainty.

Balliol reigned for four years but ran into trouble in the first month. The Scots nicknamed him 'Toom Tabard', a tabard being an outer garment worn to protect armour and often, when worn by heralds, emblazoned with someone else's coat-of-arms. 'Toom' means 'empty'. His first folly was to alienate the Macduffs, and it was soon followed by a revolt by his subjects against having to pay for one of Edward's expeditions against Galloway. The revolt never became a military rebellion, but in 1295, when Edward I was at war with France, and had an insurrection in Wales to contend with, Balliol signed a defensive alliance with France. A Franco-Scottish understanding had been in force in the past but had never been formal; this one in 1295 was the precursor of many a military alliance. In 1296 there were two Scottish invasions of Northumberland and Cumberland; they were ineffective, but Balliol, hoping to marry his son to the daughter of the King of France, and knowing that Llewellyn of Wales was also staging a rising with every hope of French aid, looked on the future with confidence. Therefore, when summoned to Newcastle to explain himself to his feudal overlord, he lightheartedly ignored the request, but he underestimated his overlord. Edward was in no hurry. He dealt with his Welsh problems, but deferred his campaign in Gascony to a later date. In 1296 he was ready for Balliol.

Berwick, now such a peaceful town, has seen many horrifying scenes, but few can have equalled that in 1296. Edward descended on it with devastating speed both by land and sea. His Welsh campaign had made him a master of this sort of combined operation. Berwick was the chief port and most prestigious border fortress of Scotland; Edward was therefore prepared to make an example of it and eliminate any further rebellious thoughts in the area. It may be argued that a swift bloody massacre at a key point ultimately saves lives because it prevents the endless dribble of casualties that occurs with a protracted resistance; but the sacking of Berwick cannot be excused even on that score. Not only the garrison but also the population of Berwick was put to the sword, a total said to be near eight thousand. Rather than eliminating long-term resistance elsewhere, it probably stimulated it. Medieval warriors often made this mistake. Brutality in one area often caused the inhabitants of another to fight with what has aptly been called 'the desperation of the doomed'. The response might be delayed for a year or more but ultimately it came – with greater emphasis.

Balliol, having refused to meet Edward before the capture of Berwick now sent him a message in which he renounced all allegiance. As Balliol had just alienated Bruce by depriving him of the lands at Annandale, his position was even weaker than it need have been. Edward moved on to Dunbar where, on 27 April 1296, the Scottish army was so disorganized that resistance was negligible. The occasion was called the Battle of Dunbar, and took place at Spott burn, two miles south of the town, but never in fact became a full-stage encounter. As Edward's vanguard approached, under the command of John de Warenne, the Scots engaged it half-heartedly. Before the main body of Edward's army had arrived they decided to break off the fight and leave the field. It was a classic example of a potentially strong army being humiliated because it lacked leadership and proper motivation. But what could be expected when a puppet king, already discredited, put a disorganized army into the field to challenge one of the most experienced and battle-hardened forces in Europe? Inevitably the surrender of the castles at Edinburgh, Roxburgh, Stirling, and Perth soon followed. Finally, Balliol himself submitted by presenting himself in simple clothing and carrying a white rod. Edward pressed on to Elgin but was magnanimous in his easy victory. He issued a general amnesty and affirmed that none of Scotland's laws should be changed. Nevertheless, he carried off the 'Stone of Destiny' from Scone, and installed it in Westminster Abbey under the Coronation Chair. At Edinburgh he was said to have picked up the famous Holy Rood, a crucifix brought there by St Margaret, and judged to be the most holy relic in Scotland. This latter act seems highly improbable for Edward was neither impious nor a fool but the story, impossible to disprove, would be excellent for rousing Scottish religious indignation.

There was, however, no need of additional refinement to stir Scottish feelings against Edward and his army. Before setting off for the postponed expedition in Gascony, taking the bulk of his army with him, he had appointed three Englishmen to administer Scotland: John de Warenne, victor of Dunbar, as Governor, Hugh de Cressingham as Treasurer, and William Ormsby as Chief Justice. The stage was now set for a series of battles which would continue intermittently for the next five hundred years.

# THE BATTLE OF
# STIRLING BRIDGE

## 11 September 1297

The situation in Scotland in 1297 is easy to analyse in the perspective of history; it was probably incomprehensible at the time. Edward had appointed three high-handed officials to administer the country in his absence. John de Warenne was a good soldier, as had been shown at Dunbar, but was inclined to be impetuous and to underrate the enemy; Cressingham was an obstinate man who saw his task as simply to extract the maximum possible quantity of taxes from the defeated Scots; Ormsby had no doubt that the best future for Scotland was to place it under an English system of justice. Of these the last was perhaps the worst, for, although men do not like being tyrannized or over-taxed, they will bear up if they feel there might ultimately be some redress in law. But the introduction of a foreign, and therefore imperfectly understood, legal system will rapidly drive them to desperation.

The Scots, of course, were a recently united nation. It was inevitable that once their accepted king proved incapable of preserving their welfare – as Balliol had so clearly failed – they would once more begin to revive their regional feelings and hostilities. Many Scots, of whom Bruce was one, felt that they had been betrayed because some of those who should have been their leaders had in fact fought for the English.

It is impossible to escape the conclusion that Edward I, so far-seeing elsewhere, was obstinate and short-sighted in his Scottish policy. His unfortunate choice of administrators has

47

been mentioned already; it seems extraordinary that he should feel that he could erect a puppet king, destroy him, and still be accepted.

Warenne was a sick man in the winter of 1296. Had he been in normal health he would have been so active, and perhaps so royal, that the Scots would have accepted English suzerainty. The Warennes, whose legitimate line would die out in 1347, were a remarkable baronial family even by medieval standards. The first of them had come over with William the Conqueror and they were closely related to the royal family. At times they opposed the king; at others they served him with a casual haughtiness. Warenne had already defied a royal inquiry (held throughout the realm) to discover by what right (*Quo Warranto*) barons held certain lands. When the Sheriff appeared, Warenne snatched down a rusty sword from the wall and said 'By this were my lands won by my ancestors, and by this will I hold them. This is my title deed.' His act of defiance was copied by others and the inquiry was abandoned. Warenne was accustomed to getting his own way by dash and fearlessness, which had already served him well at Dunbar. These qualities would doubtless have served him and his sovereign well in governing Scotland in the winter of 1296-7 if he had been able to display them. But, as we have noted, illness prevented his displaying them at that time, and when the next opportunity arrived he was at Stirling Bridge. Meanwhile, Cressingham and Ormsby had been exercising their talents to the full. The result of this combination of negative apathy and positive ineptitude was that the stage was set for the emergence of a leader of Scottish resistance – 'The hour calls forth the man.' A Strathclyde knight, one who had been thought too unimportant to be summoned to swear allegiance to Edward I, now came to the front, his name William Wallace. He was one of the Britons from Wales who had settled in Strathclyde, indeed his name Wallace, or Waleys, means 'the Welshman', but he was a true Scot for all that, perhaps a better representative of Scottish nationhood than many better-known names. In May 1297 he became involved in a brawl in Lanark, the details of which are obscure. It seems to have been a quarrel with some English soldiers over a girl; some say she was his wife. An attempt was made to arrest him, and as a result Wallace killed the Sheriff of Lanark, one Hazelrigg. This made Wallace an outlaw – and more. A man who has defied the occupying army, is a fine guerrilla fighter, and has taken to the hills in a country where there is widespread discontent, can scarcely fail to become a national hero.

Initially the rising was not a success but that was no fault of Wallace. Stirred by his defiance, and perhaps feeling their own authority would be undermined unless they took action, the Scottish barons made an attempt to reassert their independence. The effort was a dismal failure; there was no unified command and, when they met an English force at Irvine in Ayrshire, they came to terms with more speed than dignity. This was 9 July 1297. Wallace, however, was not affected; he was organizing his own army, ably assisted by Andrew Moray of Bothwell. As soon as Wallace was able, he began besieging castles and acquiring bases. Meanwhile, the English army which had been so successful at Irvine had now decided to march forward to Stirling. It was rumoured to be 40,000 strong. Wallace was besieging Dundee castle when messengers brought him notice of this move. He promptly broke off the siege and hurried off to protect Stirling, which so aptly has been called 'the key to Scotland'. There he took up position where the ground rises up to the west of the Forth. By Cambuskenneth Abbey was a narrow wooden bridge, the only entry to Stirling. It was about a hundred yards upstream from the present footbridge and should not be confused with it, although the latter gives one a good idea of what it might have been like. Its exact position may be found from the base of stone pillars on each side of the river. It was a typical medieval bridge, only wide enough for two people to walk abreast. Doubtless it closely resembled the one over the Spott burn near Dunbar where Warenne had been so successful the previous year. There, in the face of a demoralized Scots army relying on making a defence along the steep banks of the burn, he had burst across, partly using the bridge and partly fording. Doubtless he hoped to do the same at

49

Stirling Bridge. But the Forth is not the Spott; it is a fast-flowing river 250 feet across. And behind it was Wallace with 10,000 men who cared not in the least that they were outnumbered four to one. They were lean, hardy and alert, and, under a leader whom they respected, they were tolerably disciplined. They would obey orders and do nothing rash before the battle; during it and after it matters might be different. With some interest they watched the English army begin to cross the bridge and deploy on the bank in front of their own position. The figure of 40,000 seems unduly large for the size of a medieval army but, even with a quarter of this amount, the passage of the bridge would be slow. This was where all Wallace's prestige as a leader was needed to hold his men in check. It must have seemed incomprehensible to them that Wallace should allow the invader to pass such a formidable obstacle as the Forth unmolested. On the bridge they could have been held; it was a time-honoured method. Any guerrilla watching an enemy file into an ambush must wonder whether the ambush will be strong enough to hold them, and Wallace's men, as they watched large numbers of English cross the bridge, probably felt sick and disappointed at the sight. Still there was no order from Wallace. Among the English were a number of Scottish barons who had entered English service when Balliol was king. They were better horsed and equipped than any of Wallace's knights, but their hearts were not as resolute. Nevertheless, they would take pleasure in destroying what they felt to be Wallace's upstart army.

Among Warenne's army was a Scot named Sir Richard Lunday. Just before the English army began to file across the bridge, Lunday had pointed out with some vehemence that a short distance downstream was a ford where sixty men abreast could cross. Wallace knew of the ford too and had posted a detachment there as a precaution. But wading a river in the face of the enemy is not to everyone's taste; it is exhausting and uncertain, damages weapons and equipment, and gives an army a highly vulnerable feeling. Warenne, with his triumph at Dunbar fresh in mind, decided he could risk the bridge.

By 11 a.m. half the English army was over and forming up on

the other side. At its head was Cressingham, as brave as he was stupid, and a knight called Sir Marmaduke Twenge. Suddenly the Scots army rose up out of the cover and began to move down the slope. Twenge promptly gave the order to sound the charge and the English cavalry launched itself up the hill. In a moment, all was clatter and confusion. As the knights lumbered up the slope on to the points of Scottish pikes, so Wallace's archers teased and confused the rear with a shower of arrows. The archers were not a very formidable force, but they had plenty of arrows and were shooting downhill on to a clearly visible target; doubtless they were enjoying themselves greatly. An archer's life was a fine one if he had a clear target and enough ammunition, but if he ran out of arrows and was charged by enemy cavalry his chances did not amount to much. Wallace's centre, with himself, Grahame of Dundaff, and Ramsay of Dalhousie, hurled themselves straight through the middle of the English army towards the bridge. Simultaneously he launched a flanking movement which swept along the north bank and looked like cutting off the English army from reinforcements. The Scottish attack had all the advantages which come from surprise and speed and they took good care not to lose them. Much of the English trouble stemmed from the fact that they had been forming up for an offensive and not a defensive action, and now it was too late to change. Soon, instead of charging, they themselves were being charged by the long Scottish pikes. So well was this part of the battle going that Wallace sent his reserve to cross the ford – of which the exact position is not now known, for it has been eroded away – and to fall on the English flank on the other side. Warenne was not unduly dismayed or upset; he was too good a soldier for that. Sizing up the situation on the opposite bank, he cleared his infantry from the bridge and in its place launched a stream of well-armoured knights who galloped over the planks and hurled themselves into the mêlée on the other side. It was a fine dashing piece of opportunism and, if it could have been continued, might have turned the battle. But, alas for hopes; the weight of the mailed knights and their chargers at this speed was too much for the bridge. Some say Wallace had previously sawn through some of its supports, for suddenly it began to crack and fall. For those English on the far side it was now kill or be killed; there was no way out of that iron ring. Gradually they were driven back to the banks of the river. Those who plunged in were nearly all drowned but a few scrambled out on the south bank only to be slaughtered by the Scots who had forded lower down. The rest of the English army was in retreat, hastily trying to avoid being cut off, but not often succeeding. Warenne rallied them at Torwood and inflicted heavy casualties on the advancing Scots, who had now grown careless. It was, however, of no avail, and reluctantly he abandoned the fight and spurred on to Berwick. His foot soldiers were not so lucky. Most of them were baffled by the loops in the river and were easily caught; the fate of a defeated army in a hostile countryside is not a pleasant one, and it is said that thousands of unburied corpses took their revenge in pestilence on the people who had shown them no mercy. Cressingham's body received special treatment: the skin was torn off it and made into purses and belts.

Wallace was now supreme. He was elected Protector of the Kingdom and was supported by the aristocracy, particularly those who had fought for Warenne and changed sides in the hour of victory. But the English still held Roxburgh and Berwick castles and Warenne had sworn he would be back.

# THE BATTLE OF FALKIRK

## 22 July 1298

Edward returned to England from France in March 1298. He summoned his English and Scottish barons to a Parliament at York but, not surprisingly, the Scots did not appear. Wallace was now supported by all the leading dignitaries in Scotland and, to show his strength, had led a savage raid into Northumberland. The bitter feelings aroused by this raid would persist for many years, but the Scots would be the chief sufferers.

Edward's task was not as easy as he would have wished. His northern barons were not entirely convinced that, having been enlisted, they would not find their sovereign had once again departed to his French wars, leaving them to subdue Wallace on their own. And subduing Wallace did not look like being easy. Edward, however, reassured them. By a pilgrimage to the shrine of St John of Beverley he convinced them that he was sincere; and by assessing his followers accurately he gave military and administrative confidence. If you had lands to the value of £15, you were required to present yourself for service, equipped with a hauberk, an iron cap, a knife, and a horse; if you had only 40 shillings or less, you only needed a sword and a knife and a bow and arrows. These you would have anyway; how could a man hunt for his food otherwise?

With this all-embracing system of enlistment Edward I had a considerable army by June 1298. Some chroniclers gave the number as 80,000, some as 90,000. Half that number would have been difficult enough to feed and manoeuvre; there is no means of checking the size of medieval armies or of casualties except on the basis of probability. Nevertheless, Edward's army included many men experienced in the French wars. Some of them were cavalry but there were also substantial contingents of Welsh and Irish infantry; the latter were scarcely likely to endear themselves to the Scots. Among the leaders were Antony de Beck, the warlike Bishop of Durham; Humphrey de Bohun, Earl of Hereford; Bigod of Norfolk; and Lord Basset of Drayton.

Whatever the true numerical size of this army, it was too large for Wallace to oppose in the field. Like a good guerrilla leader he fell back. Progress was not entirely easy for Edward as he advanced up the east coast; Wallace had destroyed everything of use to an invading army and Edward's seaborne supply system was noticeably erratic. At Dirleton castle, held by the De Vaux family of Norman extraction, Bishop Beck's army was nearly starving and had to raid the crops growing locally. Dirleton is a castle well worth a visit, although in 1298 it was undoubtedly less formidable than the present ruins suggest. At Kirkliston Edward halted and waited for his seaborne supplies; he was not in such a hurry as to risk his great host in a country of which it might be said (as it was said later of Spain) 'where small armies are beaten and where large armies starve'.

Wallace had his problems too. Guerrilla leaders who have become national heroes may not revert to the methods which brought them to power. There is no looking back. A king, however unregal, must fight like a king. Reluctantly Wallace mustered all his strength – an army said to number 30,000 – and with this he marched to Falkirk. If he was to check Edward, this was the place to do it. Once past Falkirk the English were on their way to Stirling, and with that great army fanning out what could stop the conquest of Scotland? He is said to have chosen what was tactically a very strong position, with a morass in front and his flanks covered with rope-covered palisades. It is impossible to judge the strength of that position today, although it is easily identified, for a town has been built around and over it. What is described as 'the battlefield' is too small for the deployment of a mere fraction of the numbers said to be involved.

Both armies were in trouble before the battle started. Some of the Welsh had been fighting against the English in Wales a short time before and, now that they were in English service, were the first to complain of short rations. To cheer them up Edward had sent extra wine – an unfortunate move, for it resulted in a drunken brawl involving the near-by English. By the time order had been restored eighty Welshmen had been killed, and the remainder were threatening to join Wallace. Edward's reaction to what he felt was predictable Welsh disloyalty was so violent that the Welsh leaders were deterred from putting their threats into effect.

Much to the disgust of subsequent Scottish chroniclers, Edward was now assisted by a remarkable act of treachery. Patriotism was in those days often less powerful than self-interest or even dignity. Two barons, the Earl of Angus and the Earl of Dunbar, irritated at Wallace's rapid rise and pretensions, decided to betray him, and accordingly rode over to the English headquarters after dark. They told Edward that Wallace was planning to attack the English army by night while it was itself preparing the attack on the Scots for the next day. On the subsequent battle there has been much imaginative conjecture, not clarified by the fact that some of the accounts confuse this battle with the one which took place in 1746 on an entirely different terrain. Wallace, realizing by the absence of his treacherous earls that surprise had now been lost, decided against committing his outnumbered army to anything as speculative as a night attack. Instead he took up station where he knew Edward would accept the challenge. By deploying his army in the traditional three *schiltrons* (columns) he hoped that Edward would be induced to come straight to the charge. As his flanks were protected and there was a substantial piece of boggy ground in front of his position, he looked forward to events with reasonable confidence. Most of his army were infantry, however, and even after Stirling Bridge there was no certainty that they would be steady under prolonged attack. He also had 1000 archers and a small cavalry reserve under John Comyn.

All went as expected – initially. The English horse, under Hereford, charged headlong into the boggy ground. As they endeavoured to extricate themselves the Scottish archers singled out the most important-looking targets.

The second wave of cavalry picked its route more carefully and was more successful. But even they found themselves in trouble when they reached the Scottish pikemen. An eighteen-foot pike held by a resolute man, flanked by others of equal steadiness, is an obstacle which is not easily ridden down – as would be proved on other fields. Wallace himself was giving his infantry a fine example. Swinging his great two-handed sword he seemed to be immortal, for arrows and spears fell all around him. At any moment the balance might be tipped in favour of the Scots. But, to everyone's amazement, the Scottish cavalry, which should now have hammered home an attack into the English second line, suddenly wheeled and rode off the field. This second act of treachery was a scandal which confirmed the opinion many Scots had of their aristocracy at that time. It was almost inconceivable that one nobleman after another could desert the country's army, which was fighting its English enemy, even though that army was led by a man of inferior rank.

But it happened. But, also, Wallace fought on. Realizing that they were unable to break that wall of spears by cavalry charges, the English commanders sent forward their archers and slingers. A sling is as deadly a weapon as a shotgun at short range. But, pounded though they were with stones and arrows, the Scots held on. Their own archers from Elrick died to a man, as did Grahame of Dundaff and the twenty-year-old Earl of Fife, and other aristocrats who had remained loyal to Wallace; by now the Scots were fighting behind a wall of dead bodies. Wallace had to be dragged from the battlefield and put on a horse, but even the horse was so wounded it could carry him only a short distance. It was a bitter day in Scottish history, a mixture of shame for the treachery which had lost the battle, and pride for the staunch resistance of those who proved that Scots could not merely fight in attacks or in loose order but could also hold on after betrayal and see the battle to the end, however grim that end might be. And the battle also said much for the qualities of the English, Welsh, and Irish of Edward's army who could fight with such relentless persistence after days of near starvation and nights of perpetual alarms. The casualties are not known; one chronicler gave them as 60,000 which is probably twice as many as the entire number of men in the field in both armies; they were probably about 2,000.

Wallace was never able to raise another field army. Soon after Falkirk he resigned his post as Guardian. His achievement was, nevertheless, considerable. He had shown that it was possible to raise a truly Scottish force, that he personally could triumph over almost any odds but treachery from his own side, and that Scots could fight in both offensive and defensive warfare. After Falkirk Edward laid the country waste but then withdrew. Comyn, de Soulis, Bruce, and Lamberton became Guardians. Wallace tried desperately to organize further resistance to English domination, even going to France to enlist support. But seven years after Falkirk the Guardians handed him over to Edward. Edward respected Wallace as a warrior but was in no doubt of the danger he constituted as a symbol of national resistance. In the barbaric custom of the day Wallace was hanged, drawn, and quartered. His offence was treason – although he had never sworn fealty. But he was too dangerous a man to live. And, of course, Edward could never forgive that raid in 1297 when, after Stirling Bridge, Wallace had devastated Northumberland.

# THE BATTLE OF
# BANNOCKBURN

# 24 June 1314

After Wallace's death in 1305 it might have seemed that there would be no further 'trouble' from Scotland. Other people's viewpoints are usually difficult, and sometimes impossible, to comprehend; Edward could not understand why a militant Scot should not join the rest of the inhabitants of the British Isles and find a fortune in France; even more incomprehensible was why a Scot who had once served in the English army should no longer do so. But that was what happened. Robert Bruce, grandson of the one who had opposed Balliol in 1292, was a disappointed man. He had hoped that when Balliol had been deposed he might have been offered the Scottish crown. But he was not. Worse, he was suspected of having plotted with Bishop Lamberton who had commanded part of Wallace's army at Falkirk. It was clear to Bruce and to several of his friends and enemies that there was only one place in which he could be safe and that was on the Scottish throne. It was not an impossible ambition. One obstacle was that he needed the support of Comyn, and Comyn, the joint Guardian, had a slightly stronger claim to the throne than Bruce, although he was not stressing it. This led to an obscure and discreditable event of which the repercussions were long lasting. Bruce and Comyn, who were in Dundee on legal duty, decided to have a meeting in the privacy of the Greyfriars convent. Bruce then tried to persuade Comyn to support his bid for the throne, but failed. Tempers flared and in his rage Bruce drew dagger and stabbed Comyn in front of the altar. It may have been an unpremeditated

murder but it was a very convenient one for Bruce. Now he was
next in line for the throne. There was no looking back; supported
by a meagre army, he had himself crowned at Scone on 27 March
1306. But opposed as he was by the might of Edward I and detested by the relatives and followers of Comyn, his chances looked
slim enough.

In 1307 he made some headway. At Loudon Hill, in Ayrshire he
opposed a marauding English force commanded by the Earl of
Pembroke. His force amounted to a thousand, of which six hundred were pikemen. But they were enough. The English cavalry
charged recklessly on to the spears and became confused and
galloped off. Bruce had won an open battle; it was his first
success. Previously he had been defeated by the same Earl at
Methven and subsequently chased around the hills with a price
on his head. But now he had put his former conqueror to flight.

Fortunately for Bruce, Edward I died in the same year. The
'Hammer of the Scots' had made his son, Edward II swear he
would pursue the campaign against Bruce, even ordering him to
carry his father's coffin with the army, 'for even his bones would
make the Scots quake'. But Edward II was not interested in wars,
although he could fight when he had to. He wanted the joys of
kingship, not the ardours of a campaign. He gave token assent to
his father's wishes by taking the army into Ayrshire, but had no
heart for the task. After a few abortive skirmishes he announced
that he must return to London for his father's funeral. This gave
him an excuse to abandon the campaign and disband the army.

Nothing could have suited Bruce better. He consolidated his
own position around Aberdeen and even conquered Galloway,
where there had been strong support for the Comyns. It was now
clear to Edward II that unless he took drastic action immediately
Scotland would be lost to him for ever. Now, Edward was a
curious mixture of indolence and activity, competence and
inefficiency. On the occasions he roused himself he could be a
powerful figure, but, having taken a step or two in the manner of
his father, he would become bored and abandon the enterprise. In
1310 he decided that Bruce must be taken to task, and in conse-

quence led an army on a sweeping tour through Roxburgh, Biggar, Renfrew, and Lithgow. By the time he reached Berwick, however, he could claim nothing, for he had encountered no enemies except boredom and famine. He planned to return to Scotland in 1311 but had too many troubles at home; in consequence Bruce was able to lead a long foraging raid into Durham.

Soon afterwards the castles of Roxburgh, Dumfries, and Edinburgh also fell to Bruce. Stirling was now the only English-held castle in Scotland and even that was besieged by Robert Bruce's brother, Edward Bruce. In November 1313 Stirling castle was severely pressed though not in real danger of falling. The Governor, Sir Philip de Mowbray, being extremely weary of the siege, which seemed more of a nuisance than a danger, and knowing Edward II had every intention of returning to Scotland, with an enormous army, agreed to surrender the castle if it were not relieved by 24 June of the following year. It was a typical medieval gesture, and extremely sensible, for it relieved both sides of having to conduct an arduous and exhausting struggle. To the Scots it was an acceptable face-saving bargain, for they too were tired of the siege and of being tied down in one spot. It was, however, unlikely that Bruce would risk his slender army against a force of the size Edward might next bring against him, so it looked as if the English might be getting the better of the bargain. Nobody could have foreseen what did in fact occur.

Early in 1314 Edward ordered out the levies of all the northern counties and also of Wales and Ireland. This was a formidable force, numbering probably 25,000. Contemporary accounts stated it was twice the size of the Scottish army and that it numbered 100,000. This is clearly an exaggeration but there is a tendency nowadays to cut medieval figures a little too drastically. Sometimes the 'army' included large numbers of followers who were non-combatants until a battle was nearly over but they were nevertheless a part of the force just as much as the others. In fact, as they worked on the camp chores and transport they were vital to the efficiency of the fighting men.

Assuming Edward's numbers were 25,000, this can be broken

down into cavalry, about 5,000, archers about 8,000 and infantry (spearmen) about 12,000. The baggage train was enormous. On occasions it carried siege equipment, such as rams, bores, picks, catapults, and trebuchets; this one lumbered along with camp furniture, varied food, and all sorts of luxuries which the aristocracy thought would be pleasant to have in the field.

The Scottish army was of a very different character, but from necessity rather than from choice. Bruce was short of archers, and probably did not muster more than 2,000. He had a high proportion of light cavalry, about 2,000 in all. These lacked the heavy armour and trappings of their opponents, and would be swept away in a straightforward cavalry battle, but on rough ground or where rapid manoeuvre was essential, had many advantages. The remainder of the Scottish army was made up of spearmen, who carried the long lance, and sometimes an axe as well. Each man had a dirk which had been his constant companion since childhood though, of course, mainly used for hunting, skinning animals, and woodcraft. The spearmen were no more and no less skilled in weapon-handling than were their opponents. When formed up in *schiltrons* (shield troops), infantrymen had weapons pointing in every direction, like an elongated hedgehog.

Edward's army was mustered and arrayed for battle at Wark on 17 June. It set off to march to Stirling, aiming at covering twenty miles a day. If Stirling castle was not to be surrendered by 24 June (Midsummer Day), the English army must be within three leagues (nine miles) of it. There was no time to waste, but the weather was hot and it was apparently an exhausting march. Nevertheless, the army maintained formation.

Bruce clearly could not welcome this encounter. He was heavily outnumbered and he had already called up all his reserves. He was, however, in a position to choose his ground and Edward's route between Falkirk and Stirling would take the English army through a number of places where the ground advantage might even out the disparity in numbers. And on this occasion, if there were any desertions, it seemed that they might occur on the English side, for numerous Scots had enrolled in the English army. Bruce's position, although not good, was by no means hopeless.

Although it was somewhat of a risk, Bruce decided to let the English army come close up to Stirling. The exact site of the battle is not known, because the countryside has changed considerably over the last five hundred years. Nevertheless, it is possible to be approximately right. The National Trust for Scotland has established a memorial in the battlefield area and in the nearby centre provides a most illuminating 'tableau vivant' of the event as it probably occurred. Although nobody claims to know exactly where the battle was fought, General Christison, former G.O.C. Scottish Command, studied the ground very carefully on his retirement and gave an opinion which is not likely to be bettered. There was incidentally no village of Bannockburn at the time of the battle, so even contemporary chroniclers must have had some difficulty in identifying the exact site. One vital additional piece of information came to hand during the last year, quite fortuitously, and this throws much light on the course of the fighting, but more of this later.

On Sunday, 23 June 1314, the English army, still in remarkably good condition in spite of its long march, came up the route of the A9 through Torwood, along the old Roman road and on to the route of the A80 towards Stirling. The castle can be seen along this road and it is possible that the English had become overconfident. Before reaching Stirling, however, they had to pass through a dangerous area which was a mixture of scrub and boggy land. The Bannock burn was partly responsible for the wet patches, but a more important contribution came from the River Forth, which is tidal and has a considerable effect on the texture of the adjoining soil. At certain times, apparently firm ground becomes not unlike quicksand, but less dangerous, an interesting fact which roadbuilders have learned recently. Possibly Bruce knew this but it seems unlikely; but he profited from it all the same. The Bannock itself flows west–east across this road and then curves north. To the left of the road along which Edward was travelling were quite dangerous bogs backed by scrub. This was in front of

63

the Borestone; behind was a large swamp known as the Carse. Bruce deployed his army at the Borestone, protecting the front with concealed pits, and the flanks by resting the left against marshy ground and the right against a small hill (Gillies Hill).

Edward, realizing that the route immediately between himself and the castle would have been adequately prepared, decided on a dual form of attack. While the main body of his army continued to advance towards the castle, veering slightly to the right of Bruce's position, he sent a strong contingent to test the main defence of the Scottish army. This was the 'Great Van', a force composed of archers, cavalry, and infantry, under the Earl of Hereford. It was felt, not least by Hereford, that a sharp thrust in this quarter would send the enemy scurrying. The victory of de Warenne at Dunbar a few years ago had passed into legend and it was believed by many in Hereford's force that a similar triumph could be achieved by identical means.

But it was not to be. One of the first casualties was Sir Henry de Bohun. Sighting Bruce he spurred his horse forward in an exultant charge, hoping to end the battle then and there. Bruce was riding a Highland pony and was only lightly armoured. Seeing a heavily-mailed knight charging at him he quickly moved out of his path and, as de Bohun went by, dealt him a fearful blow with his battleaxe; it crushed de Bohun's skull and broke the axe. This was indeed a victory for morale. However, the 'Great Van' surged forward on to its task. Once in the pits, however, it was clearly in trouble. Between the pits themselves the ground was liberally covered with caltraps, three-pronged spikes so designed that whichever way they lay one spike would be uppermost. The effect of these and the pits on the English cavalry may be imagined, and, lacking effective leadership, it faltered and began to retire. Soon it was in disorder; but Bruce did not pursue.

On the right the main English body was still forcing its way forward. Along the only, but narrow, path open to it, it was easily checked, in spite of its greater numbers; the Scottish *schiltrons* were now proving their worth. Perhaps if the 'Great Van' had been launched in this quarter it might have forced a way through;

but it was too late to think of that. The 'Great Van' no longer existed as a fighting force.

For several hours the fighting in this sector went on, cruel, bloody, and indecisive. The Scots fought with skill and tenacity on the narrow front; the English, equally determined but reckless with frustration, displayed similar energy. Both sides were now confident of victory. The Scots had faith in Bruce; the English doubted if their enemy would dare leave their prepared position if the threat to the right succeeded. At 3 p.m. Edward decided his weary army had done enough for that day. Now it needed rest and, above all, water. He gave orders to pitch camp nearer the castle, and, as it happened, nearer the Forth. The site was on the Carse, on the banks of a burn known as the Pelstream. Edward knew the area from his earlier campaign – but he did not know it well enough. The English cursed as they obeyed instructions to make a camp among the streams and bogs; not appreciating the tides which altered the terrain hourly, they became sceptical of the orders they received from above. But they camped.

It was a bad night. The English army was by no means sure it would not be attacked in the darkness. Food was lacking; the supply train had not found a way through the tidal rivulets. The only event in the Englishmen's favour that night was that the Earl of Atholl, who hated Bruce although he had taken service in his army, now attacked the supply depot at Cambuskenneth. He believed that when the English captured Stirling castle he would be rewarded.

At dawn on the 24th the English woke up to realize that the Scots were close at hand. Immediately they put in a charge using the remnants of the 'Great Van' which had been shattered the day before. As the survivors fell back they jammed the remainder of the English close together on slippery, treacherous, unknown ground. On to the packed mass the Scottish archers poured what arrows they had. A few English archers who broke away, formed up, and managed to retaliate were scattered by a Scottish cavalry charge. A great commander might yet have rallied the English and sent them forward. But de Bohun, who could have done it, was lying on the Borestone with his skull split in two, and Gloucester, who had tried, was now impaled on a Scottish spear; Edward was not the man for this situation. He had already left the battlefield and was on his way to Stirling Castle, with an escort of knights. Almost as his followers saw the Royal Standard leave the field they saw another terrifying sight – apparently a new Scottish army, streaming across from Gillies Hill. In fact it was a rabble of camp followers who, believing the battle won, felt sure there was plunder to be taken. But the sight was enough.

Like all beaten and demoralized armies, Edward's now began to flee. It was a hopeless endeavour. Many were drowned in the Forth; others hopelessly and desperately put up a last fight before being massacred. Few escaped.

Edward, of course, did. He rode to Stirling and asked for admission. Mowbray, however, being bound to surrender the castle on that very day, refused. Edward rode on and eventually reached Dunbar. From Dunbar he travelled by boat to Berwick. He had lost the critical battle for Scotland. Later, when England and Scotland became united, it was dynastically, not militarily.

The visitor to Bannockburn will find everything easy except tracing the actual site of the battle. But he will find Bruce's commemorative statue, and excellent maps and a guide. It will not be difficult to visualize the events of 23/24 June 1314.

The aftermath of the battle was inevitable. The Scots acquired huge quantities of plunder and – perhaps even more important – gained a national identity. Soon they were raiding England again, and Anglo-Scottish relations, which had once seemed on the road to harmony, were now becoming increasingly bitter. Edward was now faced with so many problems nearer home that he did nothing to stop the Scots foraging. The crowning humiliation came in 1318 when Bruce captured Berwick. The following year a Scottish force under Randolph and Douglas drove far down into Yorkshire, where at Mytton-on-Swale they beat a motley force hastily assembled by the Archbishop of York. This battle was known in England as the 'White Battle' and by the Scots as 'The Chapter of Mytton'.

Contrary to popular belief, Bannockburn was not Edward's last foray into Scotland. In 1322 he took an army as far as Edinburgh only to find himself so short of provisions in a 'scorched earth' countryside that he had to retreat precipitously. But he made the attempt. Edward was not an attractive character and his reign was disastrous for Britain; his deposition and extremely cruel murder are the events best remembered about him. But, in his favour, it must be recorded that he did not give up lightly.

# THE BATTLE OF
# HALIDON HILL

# 19 July 1333

Edward II was murdered in 1327, and succeeded nominally by his fourteen-year-old son, who became Edward III. Robert Bruce's brother, Edward, who had been crowned King of Ireland, had been killed in battle at Dundalk in 1318. Bruce himself died of leprosy in 1329. His heart was taken on a crusade by his right-hand man, Sir James Douglas, the famous 'Black Douglas'. Douglas, however, was killed in Spain in 1330. New actors now came on to the stage, but the scenery was the same and the plot unchanged.

In the last year of his reign Bruce had sent the Black Douglas on one of the most devastating raids the border had ever known. Edward III in the dubious care of Mortimer, his mother's lover and father's murderer, was taken on the campaign against them. It was a time of chaos, confusion, and misery which ended with the 'Shameful Peace', in which England returned the Scottish crown, which Edward I had removed, and Edward III's sister was married to Bruce's eldest son, David – a boy of eight.

The Regency which now took control of Scottish affairs during the young king's minority could not have been set a more difficult task. Ostensibly the Regent was Randolph, Earl of Moray, but he was not entirely his own master. The recent 'Shameful Peace' had stipulated that a number of barons, known as 'the disinherited' were to be restored to their estates. As some of them were known to be English adherents, Randolph refused. Among the disinherited was Edward Balliol, the son of John Balliol (Toom Tabard) who had had such a brief and disastrous reign.

Edward Balliol now decided to claim the throne of Scotland and, aided by Edward III, who thought he might be a useful tool, raised an army. The first Regent, Randolph, had died in 1332 and had been succeeded by Donald, Earl of Mar. Balliol defeated and killed Mar at Dupplin Moor, captured Perth, and was crowned King at Scone all in the same year – 1332. He then acknowledged fealty to his backer, Edward III.

This was too much for the Scots. Reacting strongly, they appointed a new regent Sir Andrew Moray and with a hastily assembled force drove Balliol out of the country.

Clearly this meant full-scale war between England and Scotland again. In the early months of 1333 Balliol was busily preparing to regain the throne with the help of the army the English were prepared to supply. In the spring he reached Roxburgh and proceeded to put Berwick under siege. Edward joined in in person, laughed French protests to scorn, and scattered a French fleet which tried to supply the beleaguered garrison. This was an unlucky time for the Scots for they lost Sir William Douglas, famous as 'the Knight of Liddesdale', and Sir Andrew Moray, the Regent, in two separate skirmishes. But worse was to come. The new Regent was Sir Archibald Douglas and he decided that relieving Berwick was a task of the highest priority. Collecting all the men he could muster he set off to Northumberland in the early summer of 1333.

On arriving at the north side of Berwick, Douglas quickly realized he had set himself too large a task. For a while his not very substantial force tried to harry the besiegers who were pounding the walls with catapults. Their effect on the English army was negligible and partly out of frustration but partly in the hope of drawing the English army from the town they set off on a trail of devastation and burning through Northumberland. The English were not deceived, for it had already been agreed that, unless the town was relieved by a day which would later be specified, it would capitulate. Hostages were sent to ensure this.

With inexplicable stupidity – perhaps due to his youth and inexperience – Edward decided to try to frighten the town into a quick surrender, in spite of the presence of the Scottish army, by threatening to hang the son of Sir Andrew Seton, the Scottish Governor of Berwick. Seton had greatly annoyed him by resisting stubbornly and also by managing to burn part of the English blockading fleet. Seton was unmoved by the threat, and his son, young Thomas Seton, was hanged in full view of the defenders. This barbarous act did not hasten the surrender, but it caused 19 July to be specified as the agreed date.

The Scottish army, hearing this bad news, decided to call off its foraging and make one last attempt to relieve the town. It hastened back to Duns (the birthplace of Duns Scotus, the famous medieval scholar), where Douglas and the Scottish army were within easy reach of Berwick – or so it seemed. Meanwhile, Edward had posted the whole of his army, apart from a token siege force, on the hill two miles north-west of Berwick. As the A6105 runs straight through the middle of this battlefield which is also marked by a roadside plaque, it could not be much easier to find. Here Edward, who commanded the centre, was able to keep an eye both on Berwick and the approaches from Duns. The hill is 600 ft. high and slopes gently, with a hollow just short of the road, down to a marsh. He was, of course, easily seen by Douglas as he advanced.

Douglas, sensibly enough, decided that if he moved straight across Edward's front, he would be asking for instant annihilation. He therefore decided to pass in a wide skirting movement which would either avoid them – though this was unlikely – or tempt them down from the hill on to the flatter ground; what he did not know till he reached it was that this flatter ground was marshy. Once in the marsh – and it was, of course, the cavalry – there was no turning back. The English were still holding their fire and there was an air of unreality about the scene. The Scottish men-at-arms dismounted and were joined by the infantry who should have been more at home on soft ground. When they were well mixed together and moving slowly through the soggy country the English bowmen opened up.

It was not such a fusillade as would be seen later at Crécy, Poitiers, and Agincourt, but it was a foretaste, and it was enough.

The English army had just become aware of the power of the bow and were prepared and organized to make the sacrifices – of other people's time – to use it. For the longbow needed practice; it had a 70 lb pull and a small or sick man could not use it. In later years an archer would loose twelve arrows a minute, but now three or four were enough. The Scots had nothing to match it. Their cavalry were immobilized by being separated from their horses, and as the men-at-arms and knights tried to lumber up the long hill they made superb targets. The remainder, the pikemen and archers, were at a hopeless disadvantage. The pikemen could not come to grips at all, and were mostly slaughtered where they stood; the archers were trying to aim up-hill at a blind target. A few Scots did in fact climb that long grinding slope but they were promptly killed for all their bravery and trouble. Finally with cruel precision the English knights, who had been waiting in the wings, thundered across the slope and speared the Scots who had struggled out of the swamp and were trying to rally for a final charge. It was less of a battle than a scene of slaughter. It avenged the defeat at Bannockburn, although the effects were much less far-reaching. Douglas himself was killed and – it is said – four thousand others; but the English casualties were very light, as they never broke formation.

Balliol was made king, and Berwick was surrendered. But the clock had not been stopped, only put back.

It has been suggested that the battle took place on the north-west side of the hill instead of the position described above. This theory is unrealistic for two reasons. Firstly, the Scots wished to relieve Berwick and were hoping to slip by Edward, thereby getting between him and the town. If they had not been hindered by the marshy ground, they might well have succeeded; but Edward doubtless knew the route better than they did, and realized that they would be forced into arrow range by the marsh. Secondly, even the wildest medieval tactician would never have attacked directly up a slope unless cornered and desperate – as Douglas became. In normal circumstances he would try to skirt round the hill and lure the defenders out of their prepared position.

# THE BATTLE OF
# NEVILLE'S CROSS

## 13 October 1346

After Halidon Hill Scotland's identity as a nation seemed once again in jeopardy. Balliol was restored to the throne and in acknowledgement surrendered Berwick and a large tract of territory between the Tweed and the Forth. But the 'disinherited barons' now fell out among themselves and took sides, some supporting Balliol, others the exiled David II. With French support the latter party were now strong enough to drive Balliol out of the country. Edward III thereupon took an army back into Lothian and re-established him. One expedition was not enough, and there were subsequent demonstrations of military power. Scottish national resentment was not quelled; it merely watched and waited. Here and there the Scots retook a castle but Edward III was not unduly concerned. From 1327 onwards his main thoughts had been concerned with France, of which he now believed himself to be the rightful king. In 1337 he resolved to claim his right and for the next nine years was engaged on expeditions in France, a preoccupation which undoubtedly made life easier for the Scots who wished to eject the English. The castles of Stirling, Perth, and Edinburgh all fell to the Scots. On the other hand, at Dunbar in 1338, the Countess of March ('Black Agnes', from her swarthy complexion) defied an English army under the Earl of Salisbury for nineteen weeks. ('Black Agnes' had a habit of encouraging the garrison by standing on the battlements and jeering at her attackers.) By 1341 Scotland was thought safe enough for David II to return.

David, however, was not an unqualified success. He was described as being neither trustworthy nor likeable. Inevitably he felt bound to assert himself. For the first two or three years this attitude showed itself in probes towards the border. As it was clear that Edward was wholly preoccupied with France, the year 1346 seemed to offer a great chance of military glory – the defeat of an English army in the field and a really deep incursion southwards. Such a move would be welcomed by the King of France, to whom David felt he owed a considerable debt. The news of the French defeat at Crécy in late April 1346 gradually filtered back to Scotland, but its magnitude was discounted; nor from that distance were the Scots able or likely to take much notice of the way it had occurred. All they knew was that the French army had failed to stop an invading English army which was now laying siege to Calais; it seemed an opportune moment to intervene. It was believed that Edward III had taken every available man and weapon to France, with the exception of a few second-line troops left to guard the Channel ports, and every available man and ship would be needed to capture the fortress and port of Calais. David now mustered an army said to be 20,000 strong, which was small by exaggerated medieval standards but sounds reasonably probable. It was certainly good enough to clear away any opposition around the border and it marched on to Durham apparently invincible. Meanwhile an English defence force was hastily mustered, under the overall command of the Archbishop of York. Well might the Church at that time be called the Church Militant! The Archbishops of Durham, Carlisle, and Lincoln had all brought their contributory forces. The English force was said to number 15,000. It assembled at Bishop Auckland, eleven miles south of Durham. This was uncomfortably close to the Scots if they should make a sudden move, but they did not. The Archbishop had appointed an experienced soldier, Lord Ralph Neville of Raby, as the field commander; inevitably there was a Percy present and he commanded the right of the line.

The Scots had already probed south of Durham and set up a

forward position at Sunderland Bridge, three miles south of the town. Here the Scottish army received a bloody nose from the English van led by Neville. The Scots were swept away as if they had never been there. Neville pushed on to a point believed to be just north of the Neville's Cross junction. There he was facing the Scots main army, and he was joined by Percy on the right wing and the Archbishop himself on the left. Remembering their experience at Halidon Hill, the English had a fan-shaped screen of archers in front of each division. Later the archers would be deployed in *herces*, wedge-shaped formations interspersed but jutting out of the front line – as they had already been at Crécy – but at this stage their dispositions were less sophisticated. The Scots were also in three divisions with David himself in the centre, and, slightly forward, Douglas on the right and Robert on the left. The area was rough and marshy and the Scots could well have taken note of that fact. However, in spite of the fate of the Sunderland Bridge detachment they were full of confidence and pushed forward to attack without making use of the ground. If a commander does not make use of irregularities in ground and adapt his tactics to them, he will soon find himself at a disadvantage and this is what now happened to David. As they came forward to attack, Douglas's wing was constricted into the centre by the gully on their right. There, closely packed, it formed a target the English archers could not miss. The Scots, by impetuously charging forward, had contributed substantially to their own downfall. So cramped were they, they could hardly raise their arms to use their weapons, and from ahead and above poured that pitiless stream of arrows which for the next hundred years would make English armies more dreaded than Huns, Vandals, or Vikings had been. Previously it had always been felt that numbers and resolution might achieve victory or at least a cessation of attack; with the English archers it was felt that there was no trustworthy defence.

But the Scots had not forced their way south to be easily beaten. Battered and reeling from the arrow onslaught they still pressed forward. The left was less constricted and was able to drive in a part frontal, part diagonal attack. At the point now sombrely designated Red Hills they were checked. It is doubtful if they reached any further than the present line of the railway. At this stage the English cavalry, so far held in reserve, swept on to the field, entering diagonally from the right. The Scots now found that just as their advance had been constricted by the ravine so their retreat was hampered by the River Browney on one side and the Flass Bog on the other. Many were drowned in the river, while others were trapped in the bog. King David himself was caught at the river. Once again the Scottish pikes had never been properly employed because, by the time the English cavalry came in, the Scots were so disordered that no proper pike barrier could be arranged. The Scots had completely misread the ground tactically: they had no Wallace or Bruce to direct them and the result was unqualified disaster. Not only was King David taken, with four earls and the Archbishop of St Andrews, but the slaughter in the confined space crippled the Scots for many a year to come. The Earls of Menteith and Fife were captured, the former being executed as a traitor.

With David a prisoner, the Regency once more went to Robert the Steward. Robert the Steward, who had commanded the left wing at Neville's Cross, was the son of Robert Bruce's sister who had married a Norman noble named Walter Fitzalan. Fitzalan had been appointed hereditary High Steward of Scotland and his son Robert was known as Robert the Steward.* At the age of seventeen he had been appointed Regent for his ten-year-old cousin, David, who had gone into exile after Halidon Hill. Robert was extremely able as had been shown when he commanded the Scottish army in its successful enterprises between 1333 and 1341. It was owing to Fitzalan's military skill that David was able to

---

* A steward was a ward of a 'stig' or 'ste', meaning a house or hall. It is still used as sty – the house of a pig, but this does not necessarily mean that stewards were sty wards and thus pig-minders. The word gradually changed its spelling and became (in most cases) Stewart or Stuart. It should be borne in mind that from a very early date the title of 'steward' denoted a very high and important office.

return from France and wear his crown, and he was not to blame for the Scots' defeat at Neville's Cross.

In 1347 something far more calamitous than warfare struck Europe, although it did not immediately reach Scotland. This was the infamous Black Death, which halved the population of England, France and Italy. Whole villages were wiped out, and even the monasteries, which at first tried to provide some medical care, lost all their inmates. It appears to have been a form of bubonic plague, characterized by large boils in the groins and armpits, violent fever, and death within a few days. Two hundred years elapsed before the population losses were made up but that did not stop men fighting and killing each other in the meantime. Curiously, the Black Death did not reach Scotland till 1350, when it killed off a third of the people. The violent impact of the disease was enough to make England and France sign a truce which they kept for six years. It might have lasted longer, but, when Edward III offered to renounce all claims to the French throne if he were given Aquitaine free of ties (it had once been an English possession), the French king refused brusquely. In the circumstances, which are too complex to explain here, the offer was not unreasonable. Edward once again invaded France, this time through his new base at Calais. The relevance of this to the Scottish border was that in 1355, in order to take the pressure off the French, the Scots once more marched on Berwick, which they took, with French help. This time Edward was less preoccupied with France – which he felt could wait – and more interested in Scotland. He stormed back, halted at Roxburgh to give the Scots a chance to submit, and, when they did not, pushed on to Edinburgh.* The Scots tried to hinder him by clearing the country of foodstuffs, but this did not stop Edward: in revenge he burnt and destroyed every village and building in his path.

The following year (1356) the Black Prince was pursuing precisely the same policy through central France. At Poitiers he was intercepted by a huge but badly commanded French army, and

---

* Berwick had already surrendered.

the result was another devastating English victory. Even the French king was taken prisoner.

In 1357 David was released and restored to his Scottish throne. The English drove a hard bargain, for the Scots had to pay 90,000 marks (about £60,000) and cede Berwick and Roxburgh. David's eleven years' confinement in the English court had by no means embittered him and in the subsequent fourteen years of his reign he sometimes appeared to be more in tune with the English than with his own subjects. His task was in any event beyond his limited capacities; Scotland simply had not the revenue to provide for the vast ransom which was never more than half paid. Eventually, in 1363, the Scots could stand it no longer and, led by the Earl of Douglas, Robert the Steward, and the Earl of March, broke out in rebellion. Unexpectedly and briefly David showed resolution worthy of his father. He captured Douglas and crushed the revolt. Eight years later he was dead, but not before arranging with Edward III that in the absence of a Scottish male heir the English king should inherit the Scottish throne.

Needless to say, the Scots were not prepared to accept the late king's private arrangement. The Scottish Parliament promptly rejected the scheme and invited Robert the Steward to be king. Thus Robert became the first Stuart king of Scotland. He was, however, Robert II; Robert I had been his famous great-uncle, who was not, of course, a Stuart.

Robert was, alas, a poor king, quite unlike what might have been expected from his record as a Regent. Scotland suffered anarchy nearly as much as England had in the reign of Stephen. Border warfare flourished independently and unrestrained. Its high point was the battle of Otterburn or Chevy Chase, between Percy and Douglas in 1388* (which the Scots won), but there were many other incidents nearly as bloody. In 1371 the Earl of March massacred the English in Roxburgh and burnt the town; the reprisals led by Henry Percy, were on no less a scale. Berwick was captured by the Scots in 1378 but soon lost again. A Scot,

---

* See *British Battlefields: the North.*

half merchant, half pirate, named Andrew Mercer, took a mixed French, Spanish, and Scottish fleet to Scarborough and plundered it. He was counter-attacked by a similar freebooter, Philpot of London, who captured Mercer and his entire fleet. England was now reigned over by the ineffective Richard II, who before long had too many troubles near at home to give much thought to Scotland.

Robert II* died in 1390 and was succeeded by Robert III. Robert III was no more successful as a king than his father, well-meaning though he too was. In the very first year of his reign his brother, the Earl of Buchan, known very appropriately as the 'Wolf of Badenoch', burnt Elgin town and cathedral out of pure viciousness. The year 1396 also saw a remarkable clan feud between the Chattans and Kays settled in a spectacular manner. Thirty men from each clan fought to the death on the North Inch† of Perth. They were armed with bow, sword, knife, and axe. Twelve only survived. One of the Kays did not arrive in time and his place was taken by a Perth mechanic, known as Hal o' the Wynd. This blood-soaked spectacle had a cathartic effect on the passions of the thousands who watched and there was comparative peace for a few years. Today the visitor will notice a stone marking the occasion opposite Atholl Crescent, and will observe rather less bloodthirsty matches at tennis, cricket, or football, taking place on the same turf.

It was, however, clear that Scotland, like England, was now to be plagued with over-strong baronial factions. The mighty Douglas family could raise an army equivalent to that of the king – from their own lands. (The third Earl was known as Archibald the Grim.) The Macdonalds – the Lords of the Isles – thought no less of themselves. Meanwhile, in 1399, Henry of Lancaster deposed (and murdered) his cousin Richard II and became Henry IV. Initially Henry IV tried a peaceful approach to Robert III to check the harrying of the border, but it was received with indifference. Henry therefore decided to settle the matter personally.

---

* He had six sons and eight daughters, all legitimate, and six illegitimate sons as well.

† An 'inch' is an island.

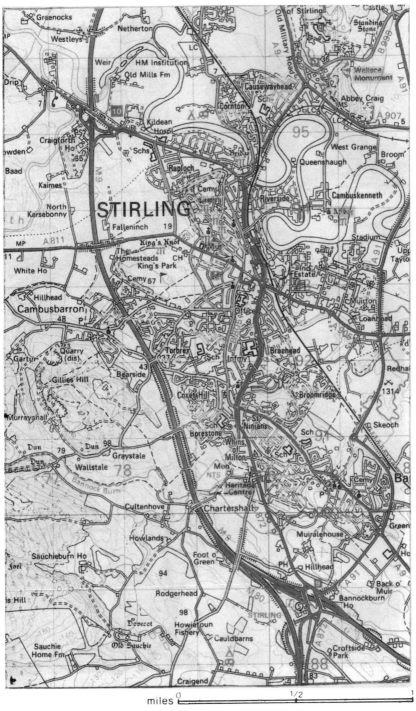

I  Stirling Bridge, 57 (Stirling)

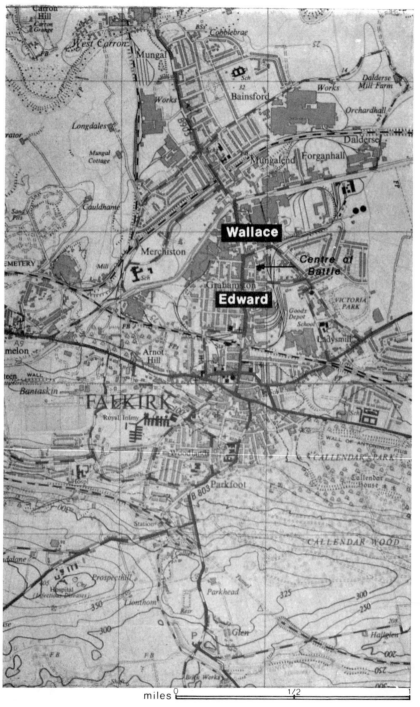

II   Falkirk, 65 (Falkirk)

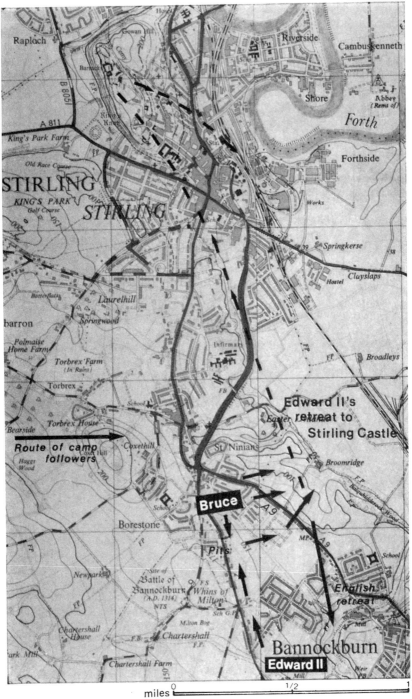

III Bannockburn, 57 (Stirling)

IV  Halidon Hill, 75 (Berwick-upon-Tweed)

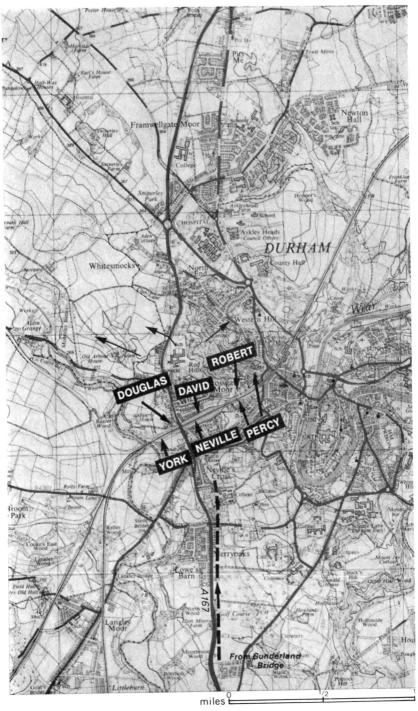

V   Neville's Cross, 88 (Tyneside and Durham)

VI  Homildon Hill, 75 (Berwick-upon-Tweed)

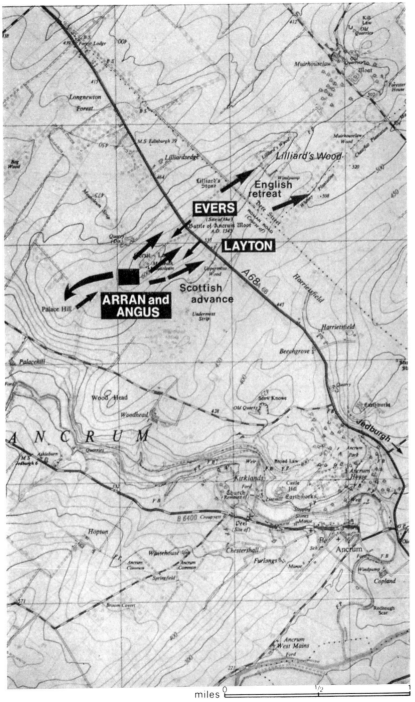

Lilliard's Wood

English retreat

EVERS
(Site of the
Battle of Ancrum Moor
A.D. 1545)

LAYTON

ARRAN and ANGUS

Scottish advance

VII   Ancrum Moor, 74 (Kelso)

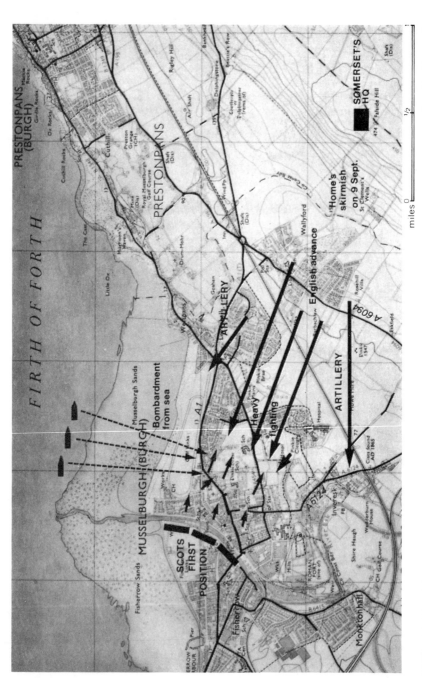

VIII  Pinkie, 66 (Edinburgh)

IX Newburn, 88 (Tyneside and Durham)

miles 0 ½

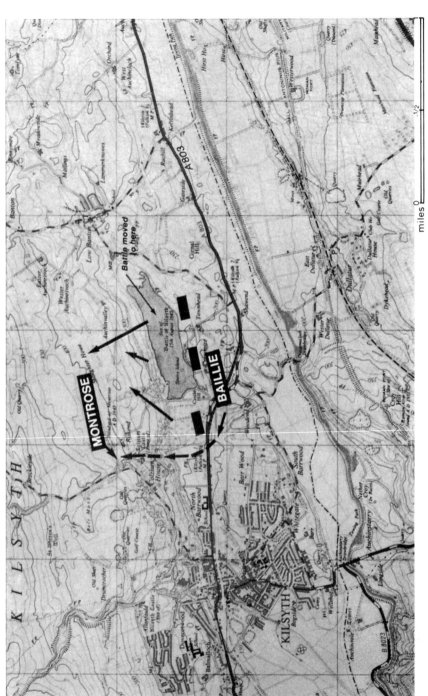

X  Kilsyth, 64 (Glasgow)

XI  Philiphaugh, 73 (Peebles)

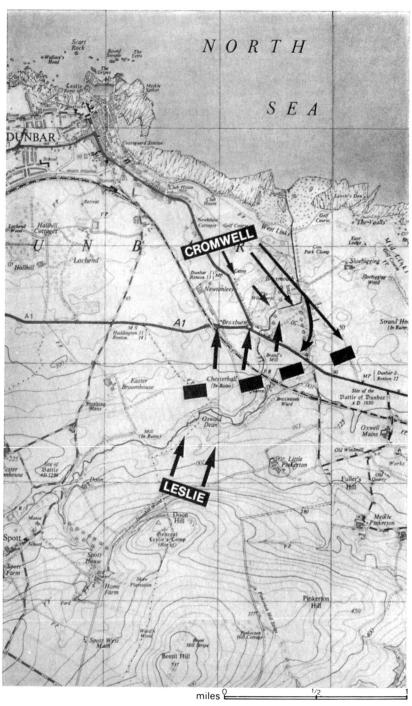

XII   Dunbar, 67 (Duns, Dunbar)

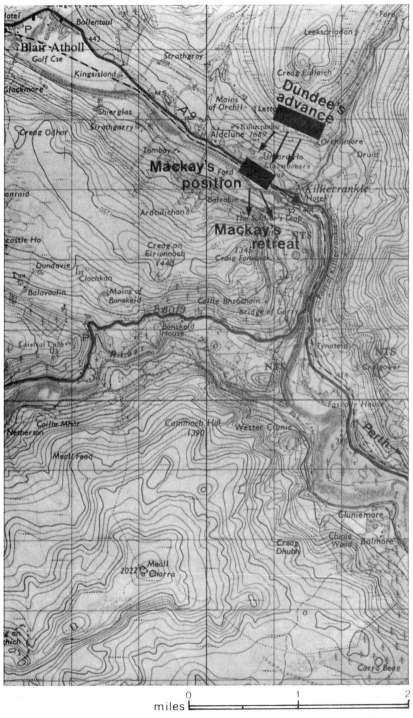

XIII  Killiecrankie, 43 (Braemar)

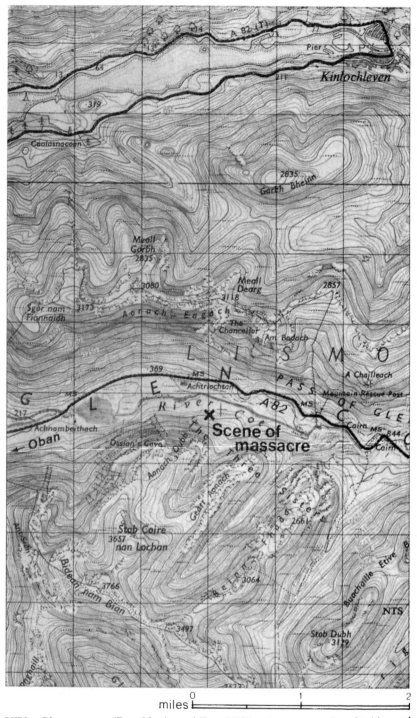

XIV   Glencoe, 41 (Ben Nevis and Fort William)

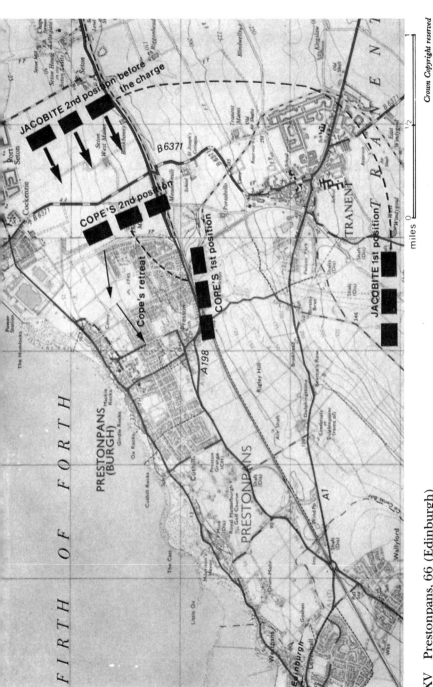

FIRTH OF FORTH

JACOBITE 2nd position before the charge

COPE'S 2nd position

Cope's retreat

B 6371

COPE'S 1st position

JACOBITE 1st position

TRANENT

PRESTONPANS (BURGH)

PRESTONPANS

A 198

A 1

Edinburgh

XV   Prestonpans, 66 (Edinburgh)

miles   0      ½      1

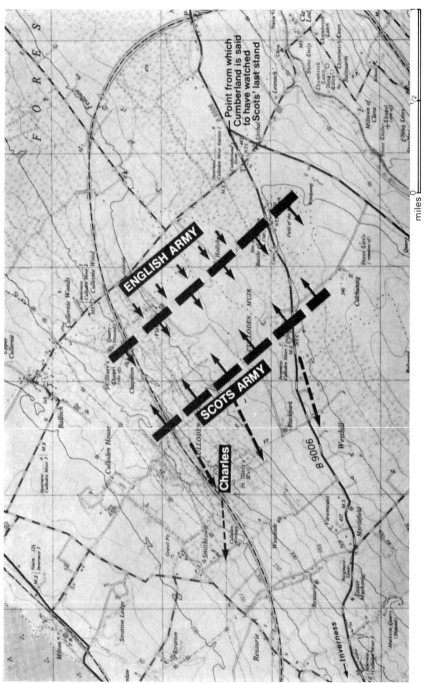

Point from which Cumberland is said to have watched Scots' last stand

ENGLISH ARMY

SCOTS ARMY

Charles

miles

XVI Culloden 27 (Nairn Forres)

# THE BATTLE OF
# HOMILDON HILL

## 14 September 1402

In July 1402 Henry IV, who had acquired the English throne by depositing and murdering his cousin Richard II, mustered his army at Lichfield with a view to dealing with the coming threat from Wales. Incompetent though Richard II had been, Henry IV had no illusions that his own usurpation of the throne would be widely welcomed. Already there had been an attempt to kill him while he was celebrating Christmas at Windsor and was presumably off his guard; the rebels had been betrayed by one of their number and were beheaded without trial. Large numbers of people persisted in believing that Richard II was still alive and even the macabre parade of a body said to be his, between Pontefract and London, failed to convince them; there were dark mutterings that this was a substitute who resembled Richard and had been killed for the purpose. They were grim days.

It was believed by the credulous that Richard had somehow escaped and found refuge in Scotland. Inevitably there was an impostor who, claiming to be Richard II, was well entertained by the Scottish court. A show of force was clearly needed in Scotland, but Wales came first. In Wales there was a guerrilla captain of exceptional ability, by name Owen Glendower, who had once been one of Richard II's squires. He had made himself master of North Wales, and was as legendary a figure as Bruce or Alfred the Great or Bertrand du Guesclin. It would be a long campaign for, so far, Henry's probes into Wales had achieved nothing.

In the event, Wales did not come first. Henry's overtures to Richard III of Scotland had received a chilly reception; if the Scots did not come to pay fealty to the rightful King of England they cared even less to pay it to a usurper. Border raiding increased and the Douglases were foremost in the fray. French privateers were already operating in the Channel and, unless action were taken against Scotland soon, there would be French soldiers marauding in Northumberland as well as cattle-raiding Scots. Henry decided that the Scots must be taught a lesson.

It was the last expedition to Scotland ever led by an English king in person, but for all that it proved a failure. Henry set off in August with three divisions, one commanded by him, one by his son, young Henry, and the third by the Earl of Arundel. It was a disciplined expedition and did no unnecessary damage. Henry moved straight to Edinburgh; somewhat unaccountably he was not intercepted by a nearby Scottish army under Albany. But his task was hopeless. The weather was unseasonably bad, with a series of violent storms, and it was clearly impossible for him to reduce Edinburgh without a long and tedious siege. Showing sound military sense, he withdrew to deal with other more immediate problems. With him went the Earl of March, ready to betray his country to obtain revenge on the Douglases who had outbid him on a marriage settlement. March had planned to marry his daughter to the powerful Duke of Rothesay, son of the king, but instead Rothesay had taken a Douglas. Adding injury to insult, Douglas now captured Dunbar castle, the fortress of the Earls of March. Within the year Rothesay was dead, though whether from the debauchery for which he was renowned or from being murdered after unwise behaviour, is not known. All this favoured the Earl of Douglas who now led even fiercer raids into England. The English, stirred by the Earl of March, produced counter-raids, one of which accounted for 400 Scots at Nesbit Moor just south of Duns. Henry had allocated all the troops he could spare to the border regions but they failed to deter an army under Douglas which penetrated to Newcastle. It was said to number 10,000; be that as it may, it was a substantial force and was undoubtedly to be numbered in thousands rather than hundreds. Murdoch Stewart, the heir to the Duke of Albany, was with it, as was young Archibald, the 4th Earl of Douglas. Having had their fun with Newcastle they were now returning to the border, planning to cross the Tweed at Coldstream. It was a well-known route – an old Roman road; it had seen battles since the dawn of history and the earlier ones are marked by burial mounds and ancient fortifications. When the English, under Percy and the Earl of March, got wind of Douglas's return route, they moved quickly and efficiently to Milfield on the river Till. There they felt they might have a good effect on the Scots who were trying to get through the water with their plunder. The Scots, however, were not prepared to run obligingly into a trap. Their outriders reported the presence of an English army of unknown size and Douglas, showing unusual caution, decided to camp on Homildon Hill and take stock.

The visitor today may look in vain for Homildon Hill, but he will find Humbleton Hill, which is the same place, along the B6351. As he comes out from Wooler he will find, two miles to the west, a terraced slope on his left, about 1000 ft. above sea level. On the right of the road he will see a large stone sticking up in the field, but he may not be able to go close to it if there are growing crops.

The battle which took place in September 1402 was extraordinary. The Scots, guarding their plunder, refused to be tempted out of their strong position. It was very wise, though cautious and unlike the Scots. But the reputation of English arms at Crécy, Poitiers, and the like had induced caution, and Douglas thought it would be prudent to let them show themselves and decide on the attack then.

This unusual policy had a not unpredictable effect. As the Scots huddled around their loot, the English army, which had now moved forward, gained confidence in spite of the disparity in numbers. Initially they were only skirmishing, but soon they grew bolder. Many of the archers came from South Wales and plenty had seen service in France; they were trained, they were experienced in war, and they had a weapon which outranged their opponents. They did not even need to use fieldcraft; they could stand out of range and pick a target on the hillside at leisure. The Scots temper would stand only a limited amount of this passive elimination.

So far neither army had tried to use its cavalry. The Scots spearmen tried an infantry charge but it was cut down while still out of range. The English (or Welsh) bowmen were retreating skilfully, luring the Scots out of the positions, killing steadily, and staying apparently immune themselves. Soon the Scots were less concerned for their plunder than their lives; soon afterwards they were in doubt about their lives too and were making a dash for the Till. The Scottish cavalry had thundered into the attack but found no opposition. As they halted they too were picked off by arrows which smashed their way through helm and corselet. The horses died faster than the men, for they were even more vulnerable. Some staggered to Red Riggs where they were slaughtered wholesale; a few broke out and got to Scotland, but not many. Most of the slaughter probably took place in the field marked by that stone, known as Bendar. This is where Douglas himself was captured, wounded in five places and with an eye knocked out – he would not otherwise have been captured. There were a lot of prisoners – Murdoch Stewart, three earls, two barons, eighty knights, and even some Frenchmen. The dead far outnumbered them and included Sinclair, Gordon, Livingston, and Ramsay of Dalhousie. More were killed in the pursuit than on the battlefield.

Percy was jubilant. The ransoms of the distinguished prisoners would make them rich for years to come. It was a marvellous and unexpected victory. Henry should be grateful.

Henry, indeed, was. But, desperately pressed for money, he demanded that the prisoners should be handed over to him to refill the royal coffers, now perilously empty. With bad grace they were handed over, but the outcome was the rebellion which led to the battle of Shrewsbury in the following year. It was hard on the Percies; they had backed Henry IV in his own bid for the throne, and at Shrewsbury Harry Percy (Hotspur) was killed by an arrow in a rebellion he had been provoked into making. But what were death and misfortune to the Percies? There were others to fight and it was battle which mattered.

# AN INTERIM OF ANARCHY
# AND BORDER WARFARE

Certainly I must confess my own barbarousness. I never heard
the old song of Percy and Douglas that I found not my heart
moved more than with a trumpet; and yet is it sung by some
blind Crouder with no rougher voice than rude style; which
being so evil apparelled in the dust and cobwebs of that
uncivil age what would it work trimmed in the gorgeous
eloquence of Pindar.

*Sir Philip Sidney (1554–1586)*

After Homildon Hill the Border saw no major battle for over a
hundred years, but it was far from peaceful. Robert III died in
1406 and once again Scotland had a Regent. This time it was
Albany, appointed at the age of seventy and designed to hold
office till he was eighty-four; and to the satisfaction of all parties
and ranks, with the exception of James, Robert III's son. Albany
had decided to send the prince, then twelve, to be educated in
France. Off Flamborough his ship was intercepted and captured
by the English. He was a prisoner for eighteen years, though not
an unhappy one. Of that, more later.

There was a brisk minor battle in 1409 when Jedburgh castle
was retaken from the English, who had held it since Neville's
Cross; the castle was so strong that its demolition was harder
than its capture. The raids went back and forth; Umphraville
captured fourteen Scottish vessels in the Forth, the Scots burnt
Penrith. Some raiders lost their way and achieved nothing. There

was a battle of a different sort in 1411, at Harlaw. The Lord of the Isles decided to claim the Earldom of Ross; Albany refused it. The Lord of the Isles assembled an army, said to number 10,000, and marched on Aberdeen. Eighteen miles north of the town at Harlaw, he met Alexander Stewart, son of the Wolf of Badenoch. The Wolf was now a reformed character, and had acquired the Earldom of Mar; he had also soldiered in France in English service. There was apparently nothing subtle about this battle; it was just a murderous head-on clash which the Lord of the Isles lost. The cost in lives to both sides was appalling. Albany followed up, and drove deep into Ross.*

In 1424, for £40,000, James was allowed to return to Scotland. In his confinement in England he had clearly thought out how he would rule, and he soon put his thoughts into effect. He decided that the House of Albany was too powerful and too pleased with itself. An outburst of lawlessness by one of the younger sons, in which he burnt Dumbarton and killed thirty-five people, gave James the excuse he needed. The Duke and his two sons were held guilty and beheaded, in company with the Earl of Lennox, at Stirling. For a man of delicate poetic sensibilities James displayed an amazing forthrightness and lack of inhibition. He summoned a Parliament to Inverness in 1427 and, when the leading chiefs attended, he imprisoned forty and executed most of them. He confiscated the Lennox earldom and estates and followed it by appropriating that of the Earl of March, although the holder at the time was loyal and not like his renegade father. On even less pretext James took the Mar estate. Draconian though these and many of his other actions were, nobody could say that they were not merited, nor vital for the future well-being of Scotland. In 1436, for good measure, he led a border raid and besieged the English in Roxburgh castle.

But even the alert James was eventually caught unawares. On 20 February 1437 he was in Perth to receive a Papal legate. As

---

* Against this background of battle and slaughter it is interesting to note that the University of St Andrews was founded in 1414. Scots were already at Paris university and Oxford and Cambridge.

the castle was being repaired he stayed in the insecure sur-roundings of the Blackfriars monastery, although warned of his danger. His own chamberlain was involved in the plot to murder him and had removed all the bolts from the doors. When, there-fore, armed men appeared late at night – James was in his night-gown – there was no means of keeping them out. James prised up a flagstone and dropped into a cellar below, but there he was discovered, cornered, and stabbed to death; he made a brave fight of it. Although no friend to the English – he sent Scots to France to help Joan of Arc – he was an able king, making many reforms, and introducing a sensible Parliamentary system into Scotland.

His son, James II, was six. He reigned for twenty-three years (1437–1460). This coincided with chaotic conditions in France, and the Wars of the Roses in England; violent though both these were, they were matched in intensity though not in scale by events in Scotland. At first James was a pawn in the power struggle between Douglas and Stewart, with other minor actors such as Crichton and Livingston trying to take advantage of his youth and inexperience. The first stage of this conflict was brought to an end when James invited the young Earl of Douglas (apparently only sixteen) and his younger brother to dinner at Edinburgh castle. Hardly had they sat down before a black bull's head was put on the table – a sign of impending death. Then James stabbed both his guests personally. As he was only nine at the time it seems that he must have had some help in the deed. This was an outrage, even for those hardened times but nobody – not even the Douglases – saw fit to complain. Eight years and two earls later, the Douglases were back in turbulent power. The internal bloody feuds of this time are too complex to be set down in a book of this length – interesting and bizarre though they were – and we must confine ourselves to border warfare and major battles. A nine years' truce between England and Scotland terminated in 1448, and nobody regretted it. First the Percies and Sir Robert Ogle burnt Dunbar, then the Earl of Salisbury did the same for Dumfries. This was May. In June the Douglases burnt Alnwick, and in July they burnt Warkworth. In October the Percies set off with a substantial force to harry Dumfriesshire. It was intercepted by 5000 Scots, some of them inevitably Douglases, at Gretna. Percy, the 3rd Earl of Northumberland, and one or two others were captured, but most of the English were killed or drowned in the river Sark. It is interesting to note that King James II was still only seventeen; the concept of children as we know it simply did not exist. Once able to walk and talk a person was treated as an adult, taken to battles, and given unsavoury tasks like choosing which prisoners should be killed and which spared. At sixteen young noblemen were commanding wings of armies – as the Black Prince did at Crécy. Surprisingly enough some of them lived to reach seventy or eighty in spite of debauchery, exposure, wounds, and accidents.

James was a soldier's king. He mixed with his men, sat on the ground or marched with them, ate the same food, and took the same risks. Nobody but he could have held the mighty Douglases at bay; with their military record, their vast estates, their enormous wealth they were virtually kings of the Border. They felt they had a better claim to the throne than James Stuart himself but they never bothered to press it; to be a Douglas was enough.

In 1451 it seemed though that James and the Douglases might still be able to live in harmony, although the Douglases were forging dangerous bonds with other powerful families. In February 1452 the Earl of Douglas was invited to Stirling to dine with the King. For a day and a night all went well, but on the second night James suddenly lost his temper and stabbed his guest in the neck. His servants then added another twenty-five wounds. Short of trying to depose the King there was little that the Douglases could do but what they could they did. The murdered Earl's brother rode into Stirling, blew twenty-four horn blasts (a sign of renouncing their allegiance to the throne), and burnt the town. In the north, their friend, the Tiger Earl of Crawford, laid the whole countryside waste until checked by James with a vastly larger force.

And so it went on. Periodically James took an army into the Douglas lands; periodically the Douglases set off a fresh string of troubles for James in a different area. One of these was in the Western Isles. Shortly after Douglas had paid a visit there, Donald Balloch took a huge fleet to Renfrewshire, burnt and plundered everything he could find, and then did the same for the Isle of Arran. James neither forgave nor forgot. In 1455 he was ready to settle the Douglases once and for all. With a large army he marched to Etrick Forest and then besieged the Douglas castle at Abercorn. Douglas quickly noted that this was not his day and disappeared over the English border. James cast his net far and wide. He demolished Strathavon castle, Douglas castle, and after a long siege the allegedly impregnable castle of Threave. Then he convened a Parliament which confiscated the Douglas estates permanently, outlawed the family, and removed from them the office of March Warden. And that for the moment was the end of the Black Douglases.

With his internal problems settled James turned to the external one – England. The time seemed appropriate to oust the old enemy from Roxburgh and Berwick. Berwick looked too difficult without French help so he marched on Roxburgh. In July 1460 he was besieging it with a well-equipped army; it had the very latest weapons – the firearms known as bombards. These were a great morale factor but erratic in performance. They were made of iron plates, bent to make a tube and welded together. As the king watched one, an unusually powerful charge of gunpowder was forced down the breech with the intention of impressing him, and the iron ball was rammed on top. The explosion split the barrel, killing all around instantly. James was twenty-nine. His son James III was nine and once again Scotland had a Regency.

For the time being Scotland prospered. James II's inspiration lived on. Roxburgh fell and was destroyed. Wark suffered a similar fate. A great triumph came unexpectedly. Henry VI had lost the great battle of Towton to Edward IV in 1461. The wretched Henry, half mad and never competent, took refuge in Scotland. In gratitude he handed over the castle and city of

Berwick. The Scots could scarcely believe their good fortune. They even sent an army into England to embarrass Edward IV by attacking Carlisle. This was not, however, a very happy venture, for the Scots had to retreat hastily after losing two or three thousand men.

Edward was not much concerned about Carlisle but was considerably interested in relations with Scotland. He was aided by the exiled Douglas in establishing connexions over the border, while at the same time the Percies, staunch supporters of Henry VI's lost cause, were steadily defeated in one castle after another. Bamburgh, Alnwick, and Dunstanborough all fell in 1462; and Hedgeley Moor and Hexham in 1464, though minor battles were major defeats for Henry VI and the Lancastrian cause, and, of course, the Percies.

James III's reign, though not as disastrous as it is sometimes described, did nothing for Scotland. He was suspicious and secretive; he chose his friends from talented but flamboyant commoners in preference to the duller less cultured nobles on whose support he had to rely. By 1480 he was condoning border raids. These had continued on a small scale over the years but were now building up into something more significant. In the spring of 1480 one of the Red Douglases, Archibald, Earl of Angus, had raided as far down as Bamborough, which he burnt. He was known as 'Archibald, Bell-the-Cat'. James thought these activities would convince the English of the need for peaceful relations with Scotland; if anything they contributed to the reverse. On the Border they were thought of as normal practice.

In 1482 James was under pressures which he seemed unable to sustain. Albany, who had been imprisoned in Edinburgh castle in 1479 but had escaped down a rope, was now in England calling himself 'King of Scotland'. What was worse he was coming north with an English army to prove his claim. James set out to meet him. At Lauder the ill-fortuned Scottish king was surprised by a party of his own noblemen, led by Archibald Bell-the-Cat, who proceeded to hang the King's lowborn friends from

Lauder Bridge. James was powerless; meekly he agreed to go to Edinburgh for discussions. Needless to say, Berwick promptly surrendered to the English, although the castle garrison remained defiant. But in August that too surrendered. Visiting Berwick today one has the feeling that all's well that ends well. It is clearly a Scottish town in England. The blood that flowed on the streets and walls of Berwick has somehow joined. Berwick, perhaps, may be likened to the boxing-ring where two fighters have pounded each other round after round and finally, on a points victory, shaken hands, smiled, and become friends. It is a town which no visitor is likely to forget.

But the end for James was not yet. Albany, his most feared opponent, crossed the Border to exile in England (although he left a garrison of English in his castle at Dunbar). Here and there James executed a suspected clan chieftain – about thirty in all. In 1486 Albany and Douglas rashly came into Scotland with a small band of supporters, hoping to find massive support. Not enough came, and Douglas was captured while Albany fled. The last of the Black Douglases was confined in the Abbey of Lindores, where he ended his days. Albany reached England and thence went to France. There, watching a tournament, he was killed by a splinter from a lance.

From 1486 onwards one plot succeeded another and James, faced with a minor civil war, took refuge in the north. Here he rallied considerable support and mustered an army which met the rebels at Blackness (close to the Forth Bridge on the south) After some ineffective skirmishing a truce was arranged; the armies parted but did not disperse. In June James felt he must now act decisively. On the 11th of the month he confronted his opponents at Sauchieburn, just south of Bannockburn, in a battle of which the records are too confused to be of value. James fled from the field leaving behind Robert Bruce's sword which he had hoped would be a talisman of victory. He hid in a nearby mill but was discovered and killed in cold blood (1488).

The new king, James IV, was fifteen. It was said that all his life he was plagued by the consciousness that he had been the tool

93

of the conspirators who had murdered his father. However that did not make him any less forthright in dealing with any of his father's former supporters, even when they appeared in 1489 holding the late King's bloodstained shirt as a banner. In the second year of his reign national morale was stimulated by the remarkable exploits of an extraordinary adventurer and pirate, Sir Andrew Wood. Wood took steps against five English ships which were plaguing the Scots in the Firth of Forth – and captured the lot. England and Scotland were not at war but Henry vii of England could not let this pass so he sent one Stephen Bull, a similar type of freebooter, to reverse the account. After a two-day fight in which both sides suffered heavy damage the three English ships were captured and taken into harbour at Dundee.

Clan feuds did not, of course, merely exist on the border nor in the remoter areas. The Drummonds and Murrays, both of Perthshire, harboured a long-standing grudge against each other. In 1490 they clashed when one of the Murrays, an abbot, was levying a church tithe on Drummond land. They were attacked by Drummonds and some 130 were locked up in a church. As the Drummonds marched off, hugely pleased with themselves, a shot from the church killed one. The Drummonds promptly surrounded the church and set fire to it. They were soon brought to trial and executed for this mass murder but it did nothing to make the two families any friendlier. In an attempt to make another area a little more peaceful and law-abiding the Lordship of the Isles was abolished in 1493, but the contribution of this to law and order was not noticeable.

For some years Anglo-Scottish relations seemed likely to improve. This was mainly the work of James himself, although in England Henry vii could not be unenthusiastic to any proposal which would be likely to save him money. James, however, was a difficult man to deal with. He varied from boisterous high spirits to black depression; he was deeply religious yet practised and condoned every form of sensual debauchery at his court; he was handsome (it was said) though he never cut his hair or his beard;

94

and he wore an iron chain belt around his waist all his life in penance for the part he might have played in his father's death.

None of this stopped him from favouring Perkin Warbeck, the improbable claimant to the English throne. Backed by Maximilian of Austria, and beguiled by the promise that Henry VII would be toppled off his throne by the supporters of Warbeck, James assembled a considerable army on the border. His reward from Warbeck – when he achieved the English throne – was to be Berwick. His army, however, had no objective and was soon brought back to Scotland. In the meantime it had amused itself burning, plundering, and avenging every real or imaginary grievance it could find.

This was in 1496. Even parsimonious Henry could not tolerate such brigandage, but for the moment he had an anti-tax insurrection in Cornwall on his hands. Encouraged, the Scots invaded Northumberland again in February 1497, though on a lesser scale.

In July, as the English seemed to be feeble beyond measure, James mustered an army at Melrose, crossed the Tweed and besieged Norham castle. Norham, as the visitor will note, was not unprepared for such eventualities and held him off. While there he heard that the Earl of Surrey was coming north fast with an army of 20,000 – considerably stronger than his own; he hastily broke off the siege and returned to Scotland. Surrey came storming up, crossed the Tweed, demolished Coldstream castle – and many minor ones – and set off to Ayton. At this point it occurred to both sides to wonder what they were fighting about; in consequence they conferred and a seven-year truce was arranged. There was an unpleasant incident near Norham the following year, when a number of Scottish traders were killed by English soldiers, but Henry cooled James down and proposed a marriage between the Scottish king and his own daughter, Margaret. Somewhat surprisingly this took place in 1503 (Margaret was fifteen) to the accompaniment of various optimistic treaties. The child of this marriage was James V; the only grandchild was the unfortunate Mary, Queen of Scots. From the latter's marriage with Darnley, later murdered, sprang James VI of

95

Scotland and 1 of England. As a king, James VI was a pathetic, arrogant, and tiresome failure but his arrival in England in 1603 did at long last unite the two countries.

James IV was relieved when hostilities between England and Scotland abated, for it gave him time to attend to the Isles where troubles flourished as briskly as ever. As fast as he executed one malcontent, another rose in his place. Three successive annual expeditions eventually established royal rule by 1506 and in what seemed a form of miracle the next few years found the clans of the Western Isles respectful and loyal to their king. The spirits of Angus Og, of Black Donald, and of Donald Balloch walked no more.

But it would have been too much to expect the Border to remain peaceful. While they remained on a minor scale the raids worried no one. But raiding, like love or hate, never stands still, and here on the Border the raids would gradually increase in number and intensity until there was a mammoth bloodletting. There were also 'incidents' which inflamed passions. In 1508 Sir Robert Ker, Warden of the Middle Marches, was, by the terms of the truce in force, investigating certain grievances, when he was murdered by three Englishmen, Heron, Lilburn, and Starhead. Heron came from one of the most turbulent border families who lived at Ford castle. Lilburn was caught, but the others escaped, though the Scots were longing to get their hands on Heron. The Scots were now reviving their old alliance with France, and England did not fail to take note.

Henry VIII who succeeded to the English throne in 1509 was of a very different temper from his father but was not at this stage anxious to fight the Scots. He saw greater gain and greater glory in a war with France. Margaret, James's wife, might have been expected to improve relations between her husband and her brother but she, believing that Henry VIII had not handed over certain jewels which were her right, showed no disposition to intervene. When Henry embarked for France, James decided that the time was ripe both to assist his French ally and to teach England a lesson.

96

In August 1513 Hume, Warden of the Marches, raided Northumberland with a force of some 6,000. On the way back, loaded with plunder, they were overtaken at Milfield by a force under Sir William Bulmer. In some ways the ensuing battle was a repetition of Homildon and the remaining Scots were glad to escape across the Border with their lives.

This was the 'Ill Raid', and it merely spurred James to greater efforts. In September he took his whole army to Flodden where in a completely unexpected disaster his army was cut to pieces and he himself was killed.* Without underrating the English achievement, the disaster was clearly in part due to James's casual attitude. The night before the battle he spent dallying with Lady Heron in Ford Castle and on the battlefield itself he fought on foot and gave impetuous orders. It is said that a major factor in the battle was the shooting of the Kendal archers, who were all too familiar with the tactics of Scottish raiders and cut them to pieces with deadly speed and accuracy.

Today the visitor to Selkirk may be lucky enough to witness the 'Common Riding'. One Scotsman was lucky enough to return from Flodden with a captured English banner, and he came from Selkirk. This antidote to a national catstrophe – it was never felt to be a disgrace, for it had been hard fought – was paraded around the town. The next year the ceremony was repeated, and continues annually to this day. Other Border towns have now introduced 'Common Ridings', but, as they will tell you in Selkirk, the honour really belongs to Selkirk – and to Selkirk alone.

The new Scottish king, James v, was one year old. Once more the clan feuds raged unchecked; once more trouble smouldered and occasionally flared up along the Marches. In 1523 a series of English raids surpassed in thoroughness everything which had gone before. The whole countryside was devastated. In September, Surrey, the son of the victor of Flodden, took 9,000 men to Jedburgh and sacked it; the Scots, however, aroused his admira-

---

* This battle was described in *British Battlefields: the North*.

tion for the vigour and persistence with which they tried to block his path. Nor did the Scots omit to hit back when and where they were able.

At the age of seventeen, James v decided to put an end to the power of the Red Douglases, who up till then had dominated his life. He did this by proclamation from Stirling, and then tried to implement it by arms. At the latter he was less successful, being compelled to abandon the sieges of Coldingham and Tantallon (which no visitor to Scotland should omit to see); but time was on his side and the Douglases withdrew to England.

Two years later, in 1528, he decided to try once again to restore his authority on the border, and hanged forty-eight of his more turbulent subjects there. But it did not last. Soon both the Border and the Isles were doing much as they pleased.

In 1542 he made his last mistake. Not wishing to make a full-scale expedition against England, but determined on an exemplary raid, he launched some 10,000 men in the direction of Carlisle. They were opposed by a mere 3,000 but, as the armies sighted each other, Oliver Sinclair, one of James's favourites, read out a proclamation that he himself was commander-in-chief. The Scots nobility refused to accept the announcement; the result was that there was no supreme command and the Scottish army fought – bravely enough at first – as an unco-ordinated host. Poor command is bad enough, but absence of command is fatal, and so it proved here. The Scots were pushed back to a narrow ford on the River Esk and thus on to Solway Moss. The result, with hundreds taken prisoner, was the greatest disgrace known to Scottish arms, although the fighting in the early stages had been nothing to be ashamed of. The news was taken to James at Falkland, and the shock and disgrace were too much for him. He went into a decline and died on 14 December. The heir to the throne was Mary, Queen of Scots, at that moment seven days old.

# THE BATTLE OF
# ANCRUM MOOR

## 12 February 1545

The arrival of the infant Mary, daughter of James v and Mary
of Guise, was bound to have a catastrophic effect on Anglo-
Scottish relations; it was not likely to be conducive to internal
harmony in Scotland either. She married in succession Francis
II of France; Henry, Lord Darnley, who was mysteriously murdered; and, finally, the suspected murderer, Bothwell. She was
eventually executed on a flimsy pretext by her cousin Queen
Elizabeth and died at Fotheringay Castle, Northamptonshire
(now demolished); she met her death with great courage and
dignity.

Initially Henry VIII had plans for Mary; he decided she should
be married to his son. The fact that Mary was an infant and a
Catholic and that his son was a Protestant and nearly an adult
did not affect his opinion of the suitability of the match; the fact
that Edward was the victim of hereditary syphilis was also considered unimportant. The Scottish nobles who had been taken
from Solway Moss agreed to the terms, and the treaty only
needed ratification by the Scottish Parliament to become a fact.
In December 1543, however, the Scottish Parliament, strongly
influenced by Cardinal Beaton, repudiated the treaty and
instead renewed the alliance with France.

Henry's fury was predictable and unprecedented. His instructions to the Earl of Hereford included the following: 'Put all to
fire and sword, burn Edinburgh Town, raze and deface it so
that it may remain for ever a perpetual memory of their falsity

and disloyalty. Sack Leith and burn and subvert it, and all the rest, putting man, woman and child to the sword without exception . . .'. And so it went on, giving detailed instructions as far as St Andrews. Hereford made two excursions in 1544, one in May, the other in September. Melrose, Kelso, Holyrood, Jedburgh, and numerous other towns and monasteries were burnt. These atrocities, apart from poisoning relations between England and Scotland for two centuries, were self-defeating for among the lands pillaged were many which belonged to Henry's Scottish supporters.

In 1545 the English were back again, this time with an even more mixed force than before. It was said to consist of 3,000 mercenaries, mainly German and Spanish, 1,500 English borderers, and 700 Scots who would do anything for money and found English money as acceptable as anyone else's. It was under the command of Sir Ralph Evers who had been on the previous expedition and distinguished himself for ruthless savagery.

At this point, the Earl of Angus, a Red Douglas whose estates had suffered badly, and the Earl of Arran, joined forces. Angus had raised 1,000 horse. The Scottish horse was small but extremely mobile and dexterous; he could even traverse boggy land by adroit jumping. The rider carried a long spear, a sword, or a battleaxe known as a 'Jedburgh staff'. With these troops Angus set off in pursuit of an English force which had plundered Melrose and was now moving on to Jedburgh. He was joined by a similar number under Lesley of Rothes. Even combined it was not a large force but it was enough to make the English think twice about crossing the Teviot without a preliminary battle. They, therefore, camped on Ancrum Moor, three and a half miles north-west of Jedburgh on 12 February.

Here Angus was joined by yet another force, under Sir Walter Scott of Buccleuch. Scott was burning for revenge, for in the previous year Evers had devastated his lands in Teviotdale, stormed two of his castles, killed many of his men, and carried off a great haul of plunder. Nevertheless, he did not allow his fury to affect his military judgement.

Ancrum Moor is easily found, for the A68 runs straight through the middle of the battlefield. The Scots initially took up station on Gersit Law overlooking the English camp, where they were in full view of their opponents. As the English settled down to their camping site, their scouts went out and inspected the Scottish position. This could be one of those occasions when the rival armies might inspect each other but not fight. The Scots were clearly outnumbered and, with memories of English archery, they might well decide to sheer off. But such was not their intention.

Instead, they performed the sort of subtle manoeuvre which occurred very rarely in those days. In clear view of the enemy scouts, who were allowed to remain unmolested, they sent followers and horses to the rear in the direction of Palace Hill. It looked, from a distance, as if they had decided that the English force was too large a nut to crack and that they would melt away to pick up reinforcements for an attack later. The sight was welcome enough to the English, who formed the opinion that a quick dash after them would destroy the basis of any possible danger on the return to the Border, and there might even be more plunder as well. Evers had a quick conference with his captains; all were unanimous that an attack should be put on straight away. The men would not like it for they were weary from their march over bad tracks from Melrose, and were already weighed down and wearied with plunder, much of it as useless as it was cumbersome. But, with a hard core of mercenaries who were paid to obey and fight, there was no hesitation. The horses were quickly resaddled, the foot-soldiers made themselves ready for battle. The only factor which could beat them was the speed by which the Scots moved away. Taking no chances on this the men-at-arms put their horses to the gallop and the infantry broke into a run.

At the top of the hill there was no sign of the Scots; and as the English army puffed and looked around it seemed they had come too late. Suddenly a shout from one of the skirmishers attracted everyone's attention. He was pointing down the slope. There, indeed, were the Scots. They had not gone far and by the look of it they had decided they must try to put up some sort of fight. Down the slope the English rushed, scarcely listening for commands.

As they came on to the Scottish spearmen it was obvious that there were many more spears than had been expected. As the cavalry ran on to what looked like an impenetrable wall of points, horses threw their riders, both horses and riders rolling over in agony. Behind, the Scottish arquebuses were keeping up an intermittent fire, picking a man here and there. The smoke blew back into English eyes which were already dazzled by the rays of the late afternoon sun. Even so, these were no novices, they had seen a dozen and more battlefields, so they fell into line and now presented three ranks to the enemy. In the third line were the arquebusiers, with the latest hand-guns. The guns fired twice a minute – if all went well – but they needed careful handling and could be aimed only from the top of the long rest which each arquebusier carried.

Now, at this critical stage, with the English force breathless, unsighted, and confused, the Scots put in a charge. Those pikes, some up to eighteen feet long, were terrifying weapons, for it seemed impossible to dodge them. They were not always a success, for a pikeman needs to be well controlled if he is not to do more damage to his own side than the enemy, but properly used, and with the right conditions, they were superb. This was such a moment. They hit the English front rank like a wall of venomous snakes' heads, sending it reeling back into the second line, which, already half-blinded by smoke, gave way and blundered on to the arquebusiers, who had their rests knocked to the ground and their powder spilt. Under the shock all fell back on to the hilltop where they tried to regroup. But the ground was too uneven, so they tried again halfway down the slope.

It was hopeless. The Scots now came hurtling on to them, burning for vengeance, and looking like demons as they whirled their claymores.

At this moment the Scottish renegades with the English army

decided this was an appropriate moment to change sides. All they had to do was to tear off the red badge they wore, shout a Scottish battlecry and plunge their swords into the nearest Englishmen. In the general tumult at the end of the battle no one would bother to question where they had come from. They were Scots and they had fought on the winning side. Who would want to challenge them?

The 'English', two-thirds of them being Spanish or German, were now in full flight. As evening drew in, for it was only February, the fugitives, singly or in bands, tried to make their escape. As usual, the local peasantry were hanging around the edges of the battlefield, happy to do business with the victors and finish off the wounded whichever side won. Now they had their chance. Some of the fiercest opponents of the flying Englishmen were the Scottish women. Although Scottish women's amiability had been commented on, with surprise, by both Roman and French, it did not extend to appreciating being raped by Border raiders. Now they took their revenge. One of the fiercest of the Scottish women, who took part in the battle itself when her lover was killed, was the 'Maiden of Lilliard', who gave her name to Lilliard's Wood, just to the north-east of the battlefield. Sir Ralph Evers was killed, as was also Sir George Layton, the cavalry commander; both were buried in Melrose Abbey with full military honours. Such was feudalism! Evers' stone coffin was discovered in 1813 near the altar, but the skeleton crumbled to dust when the lid was removed. Other English knights were taken prisoner and eventually ransomed. Although the slaughter around the battlefield was considerable, about 800 being killed, over 1,000 were taken prisoner as well.

The result of the battle was that all English raiders were cleared from the Border districts by the end of the year. It was a fine and well-planned victory and, although the English could not be expected to approve of it, they nevertheless admitted a certain admiration for the skill by which it was contrived.

# THE BATTLE OF
# PINKIE

## 🦂

## 10 September 1574

The two years which elapsed between the surprising battle of
Ancrum Moor and the even more remarkable one of Pinkie are
notable for religious and political moves rather than military
ones. The only key events which concern us here are the death
of Henry VIII on 28 January 1547 and the adoption of supreme
power by Edward Seymour, Earl of Hertford, brother-in-law
to the late king. (His sister was Jane Seymour who had died in
producing Henry's only male heir.) The new king, Edward VI,
was now ten, and Henry in his declining months had appointed
a council of sixteen for the boy's minority. Seymour was President
and it did not take him long to bribe his colleagues into letting
him become 'Lord Protector' and adopting the title of Duke of
Somerset. It then emerged that Somerset, as he was thenceforward
known, was not a mild Anglo-Catholic but an intensely bigoted
Protestant. Among his other activities was the destruction of
much that was beautiful – and therefore presumably idolatrous
– in English churches. Later it emerged that he was endowed
with stupendous courage and fortitude as well. Life is never
simple.

Within the year Somerset had contrived to plunge England
into war with both Scotland and France. This was unfortunate
but not disastrous, and Somerset was virtually above criticism
so carefully had he distributed his favours. His brother, the Lord
Admiral, became Lord Seymour of Sudeley and then married
Henry VIII's widow, Catherine Parr. He had made immoral

advances to the future Queen Elizabeth when she was only fifteen and even tried to propose marriage after Catherine died. However, his nefarious schemes, of one sort and another, ended with his execution two years later.

It was soon clear to Somerset that the French were in strength in Scotland, and unless the threat from the north was checked it would become very dangerous indeed. The Scots were unusually active at this time. Arran, the Regent, though naturally an idle man, bestirred himself to equip privateers, damp down internal feuds, establish a line of beacons with mounted sentinels nearby, and train and recruit by means of Wapinshaws – musters and inspections of local district forces.

Somerset arrived in Berwick in September 1547 with an army totalling 17,000, 14,000 of whom were English, the rest mercenaries. Lord Grey was overall cavalry commander, but Sir Ralph Vane commanded the men-at-arms (4,000) and Sir Francis Bryan the Light Horse (2,000). The German mercenary infantry were commanded by Sir Peter Mewtas and looked very impressive in their buff coats and pot helmets; each carried an arquebus and a sword. The cream of the army were the mounted Spanish arquebusiers, under the command of Don Pedro of Gamboa; they had had much battle experience. A colourful part of the army was Shelley's men-at-arms, who wore blue doublets slashed and faced with red. The army had fifteen heavy guns, 900 wagons of stores, and a contingent of archers and pikemen; there were also 1,500 pioneers, specially brought to clear the route. There were also in the English army 200 Scottish nobles and their followers, including the Earls of Bothwell and Cassilis, and there were known to be other waverers in Scotland who were waiting their moment to turn traitor. These renegades were the curse of Scotland, for they would betray their country in order to do a bad turn to an envied neighbour. This was the best English army which had ever entered Scotland. It is also one of the best documented, for the Judge-Marshall who accompanied the expedition left a diary giving the main dispositions and commanders. The army marched north up the coast, accompanied off shore by a fleet consisting of thirty warships and thirty-two transports. No opposition was encountered on the way, although there were various defiles where it might well have been badly mauled. The Earl of Warwick led the van, Somerset the centre, and Lord Dacre of Gillesland the rear. Each column had a cavalry screen at the side, pioneers out in front, and artillery at the rear. They were in no hurry and they burnt the countryside as they passed through it, in the mindless way that armies had at this time; such practices had no effect on the enemy but merely destroyed potential supplies which might have been needed later. At Longniddry, Somerset renewed contact with his fleet which was in Leith Roads; it then returned and stood off the Esk estuary. Somerset then moved down the west to Falside Hill (it was then Fawside) where he camped. Here he could see an enormous Scottish army which had taken station on the west of the Esk, on a slope known as Edmondstone Edge. The numbers in Arran's army were said to be 36,000; although probably not as large as this it was more numerous than Somerset's but not as well co-ordinated or armed; a fair estimate of its numbers would be 23,000. Somerset's first position had the left on the Forth estuary and the right on a dangerous bog. The Esk was deeper than it is now, broader and faster-flowing. The only means of crossing it was the old Roman bridge, which may still be seen. The Scottish left flank had gun positions to cover attack from sea or land. It was an excellent position for barring an advance on Edinburgh.

But, as a Scotsman once sadly recorded, most of Scotland's lost battles have been due either to treason by their nobility or imbecility by their leaders. The latter was now paramount.

The day before the battle – the 9th – Lord Home rode out in front of the English camp at Falside with 1,500 troopers and taunted the English to attack. Lord Grey asked Somerset's permission to accept, and, when this was given, went out with 1,000 men-at-arms and 500 demi-lances (cavalry lancers) under Sir George Vane. In the end it was an unequal contest, for the

English were fully armoured while the Scots had hardly a breast-plate among them. Nevertheless, there was wholesale slaughter on both sides in a contest which would do little for morale. Home was mortally wounded; his son was unhorsed and taken prisoner. Somerset meanwhile had been casting a careful eye over the landscape. He noted that the Inveresk slopes overlooked the Scots position and, after a dusk reconnaissance, he sent some cannon up; from there the Scottish lines would be within range, which was not the case at Falside. It was, however, as a glance at the map will show, a dangerously exposed position.

At this time, late on the night before the battle, Somerset received a typically medieval-type challenge to stake the issue on a tournament of ten or twenty men, the Scots to be commanded by the Earl of Huntly. Warwick was eager to accept, but Somerset would not allow it. 'For,' he said, 'the Earl of Huntly is not the equal to your lordship.' It did not occur to anyone that saving the lives of thousands might perhaps offset the social solecism of a minor Earl having the effrontery to challenge a major Earl. Somerset had probably decided there was no alternative to a murderous battle, although he probably did not realize that the Scots were so confident that they were already gambling with the ransoms of the prisoners they planned to take the next day.

The 10th was clear and mild. Somerset now sent a second artillery force on to the right flank to cover his advance and moved up towards the Esk. To his surprise and pleasure he found the Scots were advancing to meet him, having crossed the Roman bridge. They were now deploying on the west bank of the Esk, on the plain crossed by the Pinkie brook. This, incidentally, is a good mile from the battle site marked on the ordinance survey maps and is just to the west of Loretto School. (Loretto has subsequently contributed substantially to the defeat of many a Sassenach Rugby football team!)

On that fateful morning in September 1547 Arran completely misread the signs in front of him. He had assumed that Somerset's swing to the right, during which he positioned his artillery, was a panic move to reach the ships lying close off shore; in fact it was a move to draw the Scots within range of the ships' guns. Hardly were they in that exposed position than the English guns opened up. The carnage was appalling and the Scots had not yet been able to strike a blow. Their artillery, which was of poor quality, was far to the rear. The pick of the infantry, the Lowlanders (dressed in white) were in the centre, the Highlanders and the Islanders were on the right, and the left consisted of eastern county infantry under the Earl of Angus. This included a thousand monks, Black, Grey and Red Friars, who had come to the battlefield to strike a blow against the English Reformation; hardly one of them was alive at the end of the day, a fate which monkish militants had more than once known. The Scottish left flank soon began to take the entire fire from the ships; those who could therefore soon swung across into the centre to get out of range. Here things were not much better, for this was well within range of Somerset's artillery, firing over the heads of their own infantry. The Scots quickly realized the answer to standing and being slaughtered by gunfire and drove forward with tremendous force towards the heart of Somerset's position.

So far the English army had hardly been engaged but, seeing the rapid Scottish advance – far faster than could have been anticipated – Somerset ordered an immediate cavalry attack. It went in with vigour in spite of the soft ground, but, as it did so, the Scots spearmen took up position with their eighteen-foot spears and contemptuously held it off. Time and again the English men-at-arms crashed into the charge, time and again they stopped, wheeled, and regrouped. Behind that impregnable wall the Scots jeered at them as 'loons, tykes and heretics'. Grey was wounded in the cheek, Sir Andrew Flammoch all but lost the English standard, and upwards of 200 fallen men-at-arms were chopped to pieces by Highland 'whingers'. Grey received a spear thrust straight through his face, in through one cheek and out of the other. Nearly choked with blood, he reeled in the saddle, and his aides rushed to take him out of action; but he would have none of it. 'Give me a drink to wash this muck away,' he gulped. He was given a flask of beer, the only drink available, and he swallowed a quart. 'I'm all right now,' he said. (This scene was said to have taken place at Barbacklaw, the farthest point the Scots reached.)

Had the Scottish cavalry under Angus now put in a charge the day might have ended very differently. But Angus, uncertain of his infantry support, hesitated. Warwick turned the scale. Seeing that the cavalry charges could make no impact on the Scottish spearmen he ordered a triple cannonade. As the artillery began dropping shot into the Highland ranks, the bowmen sent in a steady stream of arrows and the Spanish arquebusiers galloped up, discharged their pistols into the Scottish forces, and galloped out again. They were followed by the German foot arquebusiers, known as *hackbuters*. As some of the spearmen had already broken ranks to plunder, this onslaught on a depleted line was more than flesh and blood could bear. As the weaker fell back, the stronger found their own position untenable. Suddenly, as a further English cavalry attack came in, the Scottish line broke. Now their only thought was of flight; it was, inevitably, a disaster. Some fled to the bridge where they were caught in the crossfire from the ships; others flung themselves into the river where they were drowned in thousands; yet others tried the Moss, where they were trapped. In some parts of this field there was no quarter, for in the earlier Scottish advance some wild cruelties had been perpetrated on the wounded; these were now discovered and triply avenged.

This was the 'Black Saturday of Pinkie', the Battle of Inveresk, or the Battle of Musselburgh. Whatever it was called it was a great triumph for English arms and equipment, and a sad memory for Scotland, although the Scots made a fine fight of it against impossible odds. They blamed their traitors.

> *Twas English gold and Scots traitors won*
> *Pinkie field but no Englishman.*

In fact it was the defeat of a medieval army, ill-equipped and badly commanded, by a well-drilled, well-equipped, balanced force. Unfortunately, just as cries of 'Revenge Ancrum' resounded on the fields of Pinkie, so would 'Revenge Pinkie' now be heard on other battlefields. It failed in its objective, for Mary, Queen of Scots was rushed off to France to marry the Dauphin, and French troops remained in Scotland.

# THE BATTLE OF
# NEWBURN

## 28 August 1640

Newburn was a different sort of battle from those we have described earlier in this book. It was a preliminary to the fratricidal struggle known as the Civil War, which it preceded by two years. It was a battle for religious as much as political causes; such occasions, unfortunately, seem to incorporate the worst of each.

The causes of Newburn and subsequent battles in the north will be more readily understood and appreciated by those who have considered the earlier battles described in this book than by those who study them in isolation. Newburn and the great battles of the Civil War in Scotland are ostensibly conflicts between different religions allied to political parties. Newburn was a battle between fervent Scottish Covenanters who resented Charles 1's attempts to impose on them an Anglican form of worship, and an ill-disciplined army of Royalist supporters who were in the field because their leaders had taken them there. Yet in both there were undertones of the old Border conflicts.

At Newburn the Scots were trying to preserve the religion that Somerset at Pinkie had tried but failed to impose on them. That was ninety-seven years before, and since then England had had a Catholic Queen (Mary) and a Protestant Queen (Elizabeth). For a time Scotland had had a Catholic Queen: Mary, Queen of Scots. Many Scots disliked this distaff rule, and John Knox called it 'The monstrous regiment of women'. Any form of authority by women, he affirmed, was 'repugnant to nature, insult to God and the subversion of good order, equity and justice'. Knox had been dead for fifty years when yet another dangerous woman began to plague men's lives. This was Henrietta Maria, sister of that Louis XIII of France who was busy persecuting the Huguenots. She was Charles I's wife and doubtless behind his high-handed, religious schemes. This development was a great disappointment. After the death of Elizabeth, England and Scotland had been united under James I. He had been a misguided king but was too gutless to press his foolish ideas too far, but his son Charles was of different mettle. He not only thought he had a divine right to rule; he even acted on it. But the Scots would have none of it; noblemen and ministers and merchants all swore a 'National Covenant' to resist Popery and tyranny. Thus the Covenanters were born. Charles knew this meant business and began military preparations. So did the Covenanters; they raised an army of 20,000 and advanced to Duns, ready to defend the line of the Tweed.

This was clearly rebellion and Charles knew it. He mustered an army at York – and was appalled at the poor response. Desperate for money, he asked Parliament for supplies; Parliament refused. There was clearly only one thing to do – or so it seemed. He dissolved Parliament, illegally raised a few thousand pounds for vital equipment, and sent his men to tackle the Scots.

The English army which now marched north under the Earl of Northumberland numbered 21,000, of which 2,000 were cavalry. The infantry which made up the rest was organized in companies of 200. Each, unless depleted by desertion, had a captain, a lieutenant, an ensign, three sergeants, three corporals, three drummers, and 188 private soldiers. The army had swords and muskets; there is no record that it possessed artillery when it set off.

The Scots were initially vastly better equipped. They had 24- and 32-pounder guns which had been brought over from Holland, 4,000 horse, and a variety of arms. Their number was given as 25,000. They wore a 'uniform' of a Lowland bonnet with a knot

of blue ribbons above the left ear. This is said to be the origin of
the song, 'All the blue bonnets are bound for the Border'. A
rather more valuable asset was the experience of their Commander-in-Chief, Sir Alexander Leslie of Balgonie. He had
served with Gustavus Adolphus, the brilliant Swedish General,
and had brought back with him the tactics which served that
dynamic figure so well in the Thirty Years War. One result was
that the old, effective, but unwieldy pike was reduced from
eighteen feet to fourteen; its bearers occupied the centre of every
corps, where they were flanked by musketeers. They also had
pistols and ball ammunition.

This Scottish army, led by Montrose, marched towards
Coldstream on 17 August. Crossing the Tweed was a problem,
for it was high. The Scots marched on, not plundering as their
predecessors would have done, but so terrifying was the Scots
reputation from past history that the countryfolk fled before
them. Marching south along the line of the present A6085 with
the intention of attacking Newcastle, the Scots came to Newburn.
Just by Newburn Bridge there was a ford, where Lord Conway,
the English General of Horse, had set up twelve cannon hastily
removed from Newcastle. They were defended by breastworks
and manned by 3,000 musketeers; behind were 2,500 horse. As
dusk fell, a reckless Scottish officer rode to the Tyne to water his
horse; the English did not care for such bravado and shot him
dead.

During the night Leslie mounted a cannon on the top of
Newburn church tower and drew nine pieces of ordnance to the
riverbank where they were concealed amongst the bushes. The
musketeers, under cover of darkness lined all the north bank, so
that every foot of the south bank had a gun trained on it.

At first light the attack began. The Scottish marksmanship
was deadly, particularly from the Newburn church cannon
which was firing on the English redoubt. Under cover of this
heavy fire, a small detachment of Scottish Life Guards, led by
Major Ballantyne, forced their way across the river. Soon others
followed. As they made their appearance on the south bank, men

began to fall back without orders. Hoping to re-establish some sort of reorganization, Conway now sounded the retreat.

But it was not all over. A small body of English cavaliers, wild and boisterous throughout the march, now watched sneeringly as the musketeers withdrew. 'Scum of London,' they jeered, and then, forming up, put in a charge against the advancing Scots which sent them reeling. Soon they were surrounded. Fighting on, first with pistol, then with rapier, they were overwhelmed. Even so the casualties they had inflicted before being killed or taken prisoner were alarming; it was impossible that a squadron or two of cavalry should check an army, but they nearly did.

After that it was all over. Losses on both sides were light, mainly because the main forces had not been engaged. Newburn, or as it is known, the Rout of Newburn Ford, was a victory for morale. The English on this occasion had no heart in the fight. Newcastle was now surrendered to Leslie, and shortly afterwards Durham capitulated to the Earl of Dunfermline. Perhaps the most notable aspect of these captures was the fact that the Scots behaved with the utmost propriety, plundering nothing and paying for everything except artillery and arms. Truly, times had changed.

# THE BATTLE OF
# KILSYTH

## 15 August 1645

The main events of the Civil War have been covered elsewhere in this series, principally in *British Battlefields: the Midlands*. By 1645 the two armies had acquired a certain professionalism from experience; both had been stirred by victories and tempered by stinging defeat. On 14 June the decisive battle of Naseby destroyed Charles's last hope of winning the war in England. His only hope lay in the north. Here James Graham, Marquis of Montrose, who had led the attack across the Tyne and Newburn, had broken with the Covenanters and raised the Royal Standard. He had already won five minor but important battles, such as that at Tippermuir in September 1644 when his cavalry consisted of three horses and his Irish supporters had one round each for their guns. Such deeds in such a manner gave hope indeed. Montrose was a leader of quite exceptional merit; even now he might turn the scale and win the war for his King.

In July 1645 General Baillie, the Scottish Parliamentary Commander, arranged a muster at Perth for an army of 10,000, and began to march south to link up with the forces of Lanark. This move would effectively frustrate any attempt by Montrose to march his successful army into England. Montrose, however, had other ideas. Fresh from victory at Alford (west of Aberdeen), he had come storming south, crossing the Forth at Frew, just above Stirling, marching over Bannockburn, and was now, on 14 August, encamped by the side of the Colzium burn, a mile north-east of Kilsyth. Here he knew that Baillie, whom he had outmarched, must pass him here on his way south. Montrose had 5,000 men, including some good Irish infantry and some wild though warlike Highlanders. Among them were 700 men from the Hebrides, all called Maclean. These possessed a fervent hatred of the Campbells who were the keystone of the Covenanter army. His only deficiency was in cavalry.

On the morning of the 15th Baillie and his army were on the march early, determined to sweep Montrose out of their path. It was a hot August day and they were soon in considerable discomfort as they stumbled over the rough, boggy ground. Their thick buff jerkins, useful for protection against a sword cut, now proved a cumbersome burden. Nevertheless, singing psalms, they pressed on towards Montrose's camp on the high ground west of Colzium castle. Here the Covenanters planned not only to defeat Montrose but also to cut off any retreat to the north. Having discovered that a morass lay in front of the position, they set off in a skirting movement to the north of the hill.

Montrose watched with astonishment. Whatever the long-term strategy, this was tactical suicide. With difficulty he held his troops and his fire while the Covenanters struggled across his front, feeling no doubt that they were deploying for attack while blocking an escape route to the north. Then, when their flank was fully exposed, he gave the order. The clansmen went in first.

To men accustomed to leap over the rocky surface of hills and moors, the rough ground was no problem. What happened next is best described by a Scot:

> In the headlong fury of the Highland charge alike to them were horse and foot, musketeer or cuirassier; with claymores and dirks and with heads down behind their targets they swept on with shrill hurrahs, high hoarse war cries, and the din of the pibroch in their ears. Like a living tide they went through the glen. Furiously, with their keen claymores and long dirks they fell upon the Covenanters, hewing down horse and foot with equal facility, many of the former having their thighs

shorn off close to the saddle-lap, and, in a few moments the foe became an inextricable mob.

The Covenanters were not, of course, beaten by one charge. Gradually the steady front of the Covenanter pikemen, backed by withering fire from the musketeers, began to pull the battle round in their favour. As the line stabilized, Baillie quietly detached the uncommitted rear and wheeled it unobtrusively to put in an attack on Montrose's left flank.

The move was spotted by Montrose as it began. Attack for him was always the best form of defence. Detailing the Earl of Airlie (seventy years old) to put in a charge supporting the Highlanders who had now been checked and were in trouble, he turned his own attention to the flank attack. Here in a final devastating surge the battle was now won.

It was not, of course, the work of a moment. A charge might take an hour of hard fighting to win the day, but once the initiative had been gained the remainder was a struggle for victory by one and for survival by the other. Then the carnage began. The names of Slaughter How, Drum Burn, Kill-the-Mony Butts, and Slaughter Hollow tell the details. Even now occasional relics, such as bullets or pieces of armour, are turned up. There was little mercy for those who could not flee. The Covenanters had mercilessly slaughtered wives and sweethearts of royalists after Methven, branding them as 'whores, harlots and strumpets', which they were not. Civil War armies were followed by a considerable train of camp followers but by no means all were the whores whom the Scottish Puritans found so offensive. (The Parliamentarians at Naseby had been equally undiscriminating with the women they found there, but, perhaps, with more reason.)

Kilsyth was a devastating and brilliant victory. It destroyed Baillie's army and it roused Royalist hopes to the skies. But it led to that overconfidence which had often lost Scotland battles before and would do so again.

# THE BATTLE OF PHILIPHAUGH

## 13 September 1645

As a reward for his services at Kilsyth and before, Montrose was appointed Captain-General and Lieutenant Governor of Scotland. He had certainly deserved these honours. Within the year, from a start with no money, men, ammunition, weapons, or even reliable friends, he had become master of Scotland. He had outwitted and outfought his enemies at every point.

But, as Montrose knew, there were still problems. Victories need consolidation, even acceptance. This one had been secured by Highlanders over Lowlanders and that would produce its own reaction before long. Another danger was looting. In spite of warnings, there were outbreaks at Glasgow and he hanged a dozen offenders as an example. Soon there were other troubles. The Highlanders who had left their poverty-stricken homes in the hope of plunder and money now found they would not get the first and might not see much of the latter. Their families at home relied on them for food; if their men were away at the wars and could not send money home, how would they survive?

Gradually Montrose's army began to melt away. Men who had done a little private looting – and few had not – did not wait to be discovered and hanged, and headed for home. Even more serious was the departure of the Macleans, who feared that the Campbells would attack their homes and wished to destroy their old enemies first. Nevertheless, Montrose had no option but to continue campaigning and hope to pick up more recruits in the Border country. He acquired a few but they were poor quality. On 12 September he arrived at Philiphaugh, just south of Selkirk. There, on a flat meadow just below the junction of the Yarrow and the Ettrick, he pitched camp with the Ettrick on one side and a steep tree-covered hill on the other. It is a picturesque spot and easy to find, for the road runs through it. He sent out a scouting party but it reported that no enemy were in the district.

Seven days before, Lord Leven, who had been besieging Hereford, had been informed of the result of Kilsyth. The news ran through his army and caused great discontent; men asked what they were doing fighting in England while the Royalists were destroying their kin in Scotland. Leven acted promptly, raised the siege, and sent the able Major-General Sir David Leslie hastening north with 4,000 men. He moved at such a speed that if Montrose had come south with his army – as was his original intention – Leslie would have been caught at a disadvantage and easily beaten. But he was not intercepted and beaten; instead he picked up reinforcements on the way and soon had 6,000, of which 5,000 were cavalry. As he crossed the Border he was sent news of Montrose's latest moves and of the weakness of his army. He adapted his route accordingly, crossing the Tweed at Rae and marching straight to the junction of the Tweed and Ettrick; here he was a mere three miles from Montrose, and unsuspected.

The 13th was one of those foggy mornings which soon clear but make visibility negligible while the fog lasts. Montrose, who was in quarters in Selkirk two miles away, sent out scouts, but, not surprisingly, they saw nothing. The town was unfriendly to his cause but he felt he owed himself a little comfort. When the news of the disaster came to him he was at breakfast.

Leslie had divided his forces into two for this surprise attack. Coming up from Sunderland, the village where they had camped overnight, the two wings arrived completely undetected. Guided by local sympathizers, one came up the left bank of the Ettrick, the other along the road. They took the Royalists completely by surprise. Montrose's men had dug a few shallow trenches and these now became the scene of desperate fighting. The final resistance was put up by Montrose's 500 Ulstermen, of whom 400 were killed. Gradually they fell back into the area now occupied by the Philiphaugh farm. Montrose had arrived within minutes of the alarm sounding and with a mere hundred horsemen put in an attack so desperately that for a moment 2,000 dragoons rocked back in confusion. In the same way a few determined men can send a crowd reeling backwards; but the crowd soon recovers and their weight tells.

On the field it was quickly over. Montrose would have died then and there – and perhaps should have been allowed to – but instead he was dragged out by his lieutenants and was soon spurring away from that scene where all his hopes had foundered. After he had left, the rest surrendered.

What happened then was an eternal disgrace to Leslie and his advisers. The prisoners were marched two miles to Newark Castle (still easily seen but not visitable). Here they were herded into the courtyard and shot down by the dragoons in cold blood. They were buried at Slain Man's Lee, where their bones were discovered in 1810; there were said to be a thousand skeletons.

Nor, alas, was that all. Eighty wretched fugitives, all women and children, were overtaken by the Covenanters at Linlithgow Bridge. There they were flung into the Avon, fifty feet below. Those who struggled to the banks were pushed back into the water with pikes and, like the others, drowned. The Covenanters had been told that 'the curses which befell the enemies of God would fall on him who suffered one Amalekite to escape'.

As Mme Roland said witnessing the horrors of the French Revolution in 1793: 'O liberty, what crimes are committed in thy name.' As an afterthought she added, 'The more I see of men, the more I like dogs.'

# THE BATTLE OF DUNBAR

# 3 September 1650

The Civil War was drawing to an end in 1650 but, inevitably, after eight years, had taken courses and seen action which would never have been dreamed of in its early stages. King Charles had been executed as a tyrant, but the government which had replaced his was full of fanatics and aristocrats. In 1650, however, there was still royalist resistance in Ireland and Scotland.

Cromwell took an army to Ireland in August 1649. By the time he returned in May 1650 he had behaved with such ruthlessness that his name is still mentioned with hatred – over three hundred years later.

He would have stayed longer and completed his conquest of the whole country but the news from Scotland brought him hurrying home. Prince Charles, later to be Charles II, had 'taken the Covenant' and professed to be an ardent Presbyterian. (He was in fact a Catholic at heart and on his death-bed was officially received into that faith.) His return to Scotland followed a strong revulsion by the Scots against the highhandedness of the English Parliamentarians and their horror at the execution of the King. Cromwell, having conquered the Royalists in Ireland, now found himself confronted by a hostile Scotland with an army which might link up with the remaining English royalists at any moment. But he had no doubts about what he should do. On 22 July 1650 he was crossing the Border with 20,000 men.

The Scots easily foresaw what lay ahead and made preparations accordingly. Edinburgh castle was strengthened and garrisoned, as were many other castles. The countryside over which Cromwell would march was laid waste to deny him supplies, and an army of 30,000 was mustered to meet him. The army was then deployed on the outskirts of Edinburgh behind hastily but well-made fortifications. Against these Cromwell hurled his forces in vain. By 31 August his troops were short of supplies, frustrated, and full of sickness. Worse still his reputation as a general had been severely mauled. But facts are facts and on the evening of the 31st he gave the order to burn their huts and begin to withdraw.

The sight of the scourge of the Royalists beginning to retreat appears to have stirred Leslie to even greater efforts. As his previous victories – such as at Philiphaugh – had shown, he was quick to seize and hold the initiative. At this point he did so by marching his entire army of 23,000 at top speed to a point, three miles south of Dunbar, where Cromwell would have to pass between him and the sea. Leslie had taken up position on Doon Hill and with twice Cromwell's numbers looked forward with pleasure to the next day. It was now the evening of 2 September.

Unfortunately for Leslie, he was accompanied by a number of fanatical clergy who were extreme even by Civil War standards. On the next day, as dawn broke, they clustered around Leslie and urged him to charge down on the defenceless English, who were now well in the trap, and sweep them into the sea. 'The Lord hath delivered Antichrist into our hands and like Gideon you should descend on them and sweep them away before you,' they told him. With astonishing stupidity Leslie listened to what they said and apparently acted on it. Within a few minutes his army was moving down the slopes into the Brox Burn valley. There may, however, have been certain military considerations in his decision, for Cromwell was no novice and it was not out of the question that he might hold up Leslie's front line while the remainder of his army slipped past. This would no longer be possible. Cromwell observed Leslie's moves through his 'perspective glass', as the early telescope was called. 'They are coming down,' he exclaimed. 'The Lord hath delivered them into our hands.' All that day he watched as Leslie deployed his troops along the road leading to Berwick, and made his own dispositions accordingly Even with this sudden dramatic turn of events, this would be no easy battle.

That night was stormy and wet. Morning broke through rain and mist. Leslie would clearly be poised for the attack so, to put him off balance, Cromwell launched a swift thrust on to the Scots' right, and weaker, flank. The advantage was momentary, for, almost as they came up, the Scottish cavalry put in their own attack in the same quarter. Within minutes the two wings were locked together. And so it stayed.

For an hour it was cut and thrust in this quarter, the English line giving slightly; then, as Cromwell poured in more and more men, the Scots began to be forced back. Equal pressure was now coming on the Scots centre, where the redoubtable Monk was directing the attack. The day had hardly begun, but the casualties were mounting fast. At one moment the Scots were hurling themselves into the attack, then, when the tide turned, were facing an English counterthrust until they were literally slashed to the ground by the cavalry. A whole brigade of Highlanders, whose reputation lay in making the charge, not holding it, nevertheless stood and perished to a man. In many places the soldiers were 'at push of pike', i.e. pikemen confronting pikemen.

At this stage, with the armies virtually deadlocked in a killing ground where the superior numbers of the Scots might tell, Cromwell showed his genius as a cavalry commander. It was impossible to get at Leslie's left flank, protected as it was by the ravine, so, taking out the cavalry reserve, he loosed it on Leslie's right with one final stunning shock.

It reeled, gave, and blundered on to the centre. As the disordered Scots fell back, some trying to turn and face the enemy, others trying to slip back away from those flashing swords, the centre too began to waver. And as the centre gave way the left, already under pressure, began to fall back to straighten the line.

In a moment, all was disaster. The English poured through, though many a man was cut down in the moment of triumph by a Scot who could fall back no more and took a man with him before he died. But soon it was all over, and the Scots were fleeing. At that moment Cromwell's trumpets sounded, his army halted, and all sang the 117th Psalm. It has two verses only:

*O praise the Lord, all ye nations: praise him, all ye people.*
*For his merciful kindness is great toward us; and the truth*
*of the Lord endureth for ever. Praise ye the Lord.*

But triumph, not mercy, was in their hearts. The trumpets sounded again and the pursuit and the killing, stretched over eight miles. The dead were perhaps luckier than the prisoners. The latter were stripped by their guards and then driven half-naked to Durham. No food was provided in eight days. The wretched captives ate leaves, twigs, raw cabbages, anything they could snatch up, as their guards jeered at them. Many fell out and were shot; half the original 5,000 reached Durham and many died on arrival. Of the survivors, 200 were sent to Virginia.

Such was the surprising but decisive Battle of Dunbar. It was not quite the end of Scottish resistance, for that would occur in 'the crowning mercy' of Worcester the following year. Whatever one thinks of Cromwell's sanctimoniousness and ruthless autocracy there can be no two ways about his generalship. Not only was he the architect of victory for his army but he was a superb field commander.

# THE BATTLE OF KILLIECRANKIE

🦎

# 27 July 1689

After Cromwell's unexpected but decisive victory at Dunbar came the even more fateful battle at Worcester the following year. Cromwell called Worcester 'the crowning mercy'; mercy was noticeably absent from the later stages of the Civil War, but what Cromwell doubtless thought was that all royalist resistance was completely and for ever crushed. His use of the word 'crowning' is interesting and perhaps reveals that he saw his Government as a natural successor to the monarchy. Politics, as Cromwell and his supporters soon realized, is the art of the possible. Ironically, the man who had sent his king to the scaffold in the cause of democracy soon found himself ruling more autocratically than Charles had ever done. Historians nowadays believe that Cromwell was less despotic than he is accused of being, but no one would claim that his rule was democratic. Surrounded by fanatics such as 'the Saints' and the Levellers, and frequently under the threat of assassination, he could scarcely be expected to behave like a benign caretaker.

After his death in 1658 the country lapsed into such chaos that the only solution seemed to be the restoration of the Stuarts. In consequence, in 1660, Charles II returned to sit on the English throne. Charles knew by bitter experience what it was like to be an exiled monarch and an unwelcome guest at foreign courts. Once back on the English throne he was determined never to lose it. Nevertheless, he was secretly a Roman Catholic and would, if the opportunity had presented itself have restored both the

Roman Catholic religion and an even more autocratic régime than his father.

His brother, James II, who succeeded him, lasted three years only. The best that can be said of him was that he was capable in military matters; the worst was that he was bigoted, obstinate, cruel, and stupid. Eventually he was toppled off the throne and allowed to escape to France. He was succeeded by William III, the Prince of Orange, and Mary. The Stuarts were once more in exile.

In view of the way James II and his brother had treated Scotland it was astonishing that there should have been any sympathy at all for the Stuarts. Both monarchs had put the Scottish Episcopalians in power and the Episcopalians had relentlessly suppressed the Covenanters. Goaded to desperation, the Covenanters had rebelled in 1679 and murdered the Archbishop of St Andrews. Their hopes came to a sudden end when the Duke of Monmouth, eldest of Charles II's illegitimate sons, scattered them in the Battle of Bothwell Bridge (June 1679). However, nine years later, when James II was pushed into exile, the Presbyterians rose again. The fact that the exiled king was a Scot had no influence on their actions; their prime motive was to revenge themselves on the Episcopalians who had treated them so harshly. This set the scene for the fastest decisive battle in British history.

One of James II's supporters was Colonel John Graham of Claverhouse, whom James had made Viscount Dundee. When the Convention of the Scottish Estates met at Edinburgh and pronounced that James II had forfeited the throne, Dundee dissociated himself from the motion, rode north and raised the clans. It was not an easy matter. The Marquis of Atholl stated that he was loyal to William III, even though the remainder of the inhabitants of the district sympathized with James (whom they referred to as James VIII) and his Jacobite followers. William had appointed General Hugh Mackay of Scourie to be Commander-in-Chief of his army in Scotland and Mackay was no novice. His first move was to blockade Edinburgh Castle which was held for the Jacobites by the Duke of Gordon; his next was to isolate Dundee from potential supporters.

Events moved faster than expected. While the Marquis of Atholl was away, his steward, Patrick Stewart of Ballechin, seized the castle of Blair Atholl and declared for the Jacobite cause. The move came as a surprise to Dundee – although a welcome one – and he decided to move south to support this new adherent to the cause.

Strategically the situation was evenly balanced. Mackay had left most of his infantry blockading Edinburgh Castle and his mixed force of 450 was scarcely a battle-winning factor. Equally, Dundee could not hope to use his newly recruited Macdonalds and Camerons until he controlled the vital passes of Dunkeld, Drumochter, and Killiecrankie. Neither general had a force large enough to make the moves necessary to the start of a campaign. For a few days both manoeuvred and marched waiting for an opportunity to present itself. Mackay occupied Inverness and garrisoned it with a small force; Dundee acquired another 300 Irish recruits. Suddenly, however, an opportunity opened up for Mackay. The Duke of Gordon surrendered Edinburgh Castle on 13 June, thereby releasing Mackay's infantry regiments. Mackay promptly returned to Edinburgh to reorganize and re-equip what was now undoubtedly the stronger force. Even so it had dangerous weaknesses. All his regiments were inexperienced and there was no certainty as to how they would behave if confronted with a Highland charge. A good number were recent recruits. Nevertheless, his numbers now totalled 4,500 and this enabled him to choose a plan by which Dundee would be cut off and isolated. A first step was to recover Blair Atholl. Equally, Dundee was determined he should not do so, for it gave him control of access to Angus and Strathearn. While Mackay was no farther forward than Perth, therefore, Dundee moved towards Blair with a mixed force of Macdonalds, Camerons, and MacLeans, plus, of course, his recent Irish recruits. This army was roughly equivalent in numbers to that of Mackay, and probably a lot more spirited. Dundee reached Blair well in advance of Mackay's advance party which then had to make a rapid retreat down the awkward pass of Killiecrankie. However,

once at Killiecrankie, Lord Murray, Mackay's vanguard commander, decided to stay and prevent Dundee's men filtering
through. Mackay sent him reinforcements, bringing the total up
to 400. This may not seem much to hold up an army of 4,000
but the Pass is three miles long, has precipitous sides, and offers
numerous opportunities for ambush. Nevertheless, as Mackay
knew, it was not sufficient to hold up Dundee; he had to be defeated in battle. On 27 July therefore he took his army through the
pass and halted on the level ground along by the river Garry,
near Aldclune. Mackay lacked experience of mountain warfare
or he would have realized how vulnerable his position was.
Scouts soon reported that Dundee's advance party was now very
close. More ominous was the news that some of Dundee's men
were positioned on Mackay's flank on higher ground. How many
were there he did not know, but he quickly appreciated that he was
now caught in a narrow pass with a river on one side and a
formidable enemy on his right on higher ground. A further thought
was that Dundee's men were thoroughly accustomed to fighting
and movement in such terrain; his were not.

Action must now be swift if he were not to be annihilated. He
turned his army to the right and faced the higher ground where,
he suspected rightly, the main threat lay. He was able to reach
the slope behind Urrard House, and decided to stay there, as it
was a reasonable defensive position, though still exposed. His
line from right to left was East Yorkshires, King's Own Scottish
Borderers, Scots Fusiliers, and Royal Irish. To the rear, in
reserve, were the Somerset Light Infantry. (None of them bore
these names at the time, but that is what they later became.)
Mackay was only too well aware that, if Dundee's men moved as
adroitly as they undoubtedly could, they could cut in behind him
and systematically chop his army to pieces. To prevent this
happening, he lengthened his line, which was done by reducing
it from six ranks to three. Dundee noted the move and balanced
it by thinning his own line, thereby keeping his options open.
Then they looked at each other. A few skirmishers clashed, mainly
because Mackay was trying to make Dundee show his hand. A

few shots bounced among the rocks from Mackay's three ancient guns. Mackay waited anxiously, knowing that if the attack came as darkness fell he could be in trouble, indeed. He gave a short harangue to his troops, letting them know what their fate would be if they did not fight vigorously enough to win. But no attack came.

At last, soon after 7 p.m. with dusk not far away, Dundee gave the order. His Highlanders, mostly naked to the waist, shoeless, and some dressed only in their weapons, leapt forward with a wild unearthly yell. As feared, they bore on Mackay's right who met them with steady musketry. But musketry needs time, and, before men could reload, the Highlanders were on to them with the broadsword. Desperate, Mackay's men tried to fend them off with their muskets. At this time the bayonet was plugged into the muzzle of the musket; thus it could not be put into position until after all firing had finished. The Highlanders charged so quickly that they were on to their opponents before they could plug in their bayonets, let alone use them. With their ammunition gone and equipped only with short bayonets, Mackay's troops were virtually helpless. In the dusk, with wild half-naked Highlanders leaping on to them, cutting and slashing, and with no leader in sight, it was all too much for the inexperienced recruits. As the line began to crumble and fall back Mackay made a last desperate effort. He ordered up his two troops of cavalry and, cursing roundly, rode forth himself to lead the counterattack. Only one man followed him. His raw troops, bewildered and frightened, then did the very worst they could do for themselves: they ran. Stumbling and utterly confused, many of them got in each other's way and fell easily to the wild Highlanders. Mackay was lucky not to have shared their fate, but somehow in the general turmoil his presence was overlooked. He could, of course, easily have shared the fate of Dundee; but even the death of both the commanders could hardly have made this battle more bizarre. As it was Mackay now rode back through his lines to a point where the impetus of the Highland charge was spent. There he rallied 400 men and made his way back to Aberfeldy.

But it was no bloodless victory for the Scots. In those fateful opening minutes Mackay's muskeeters had taken a heavy toll; six hundred of Dundee's army died with him on the field. These casualties made the battle a loss for both sides; Mackay's army had been cut to pieces, but, with the death of Dundee and so many of his supporters, all hopes of a Jacobite revival were extinguished for the time being. Dundee was buried in his armour at Blair. Curiously enough, the effects of his death were not felt immediately. Elated by their victory his army stayed in the field, organized reinforcements which brought their numbers up to 5,000, and marched forward to Dunkeld. Reorganization had taken time and it was 21 August before they reached the little cathedral town. There they found the newly formed Cameronian regiment, commanded by Lieut.-Col. William Cleland, aged twenty-eight. Their numbers are said to have amounted to under 1,200, but they had established themselves in the houses and it was more than the Highlanders could do to move them. Cleland, who was a reputable poet as well as a brave soldier, was killed early in the fighting, but his men held on. Eventually the Highlanders wearied of this dull methodical battle of attrition which they would win – but to what purpose? To the surprise and joy of the Cameronians, they withdrew and returned to their homes. A more lasting effect of the battle came from Mackay's pondering on the reasons why he lost it. A year later he invented a type of bayonet which did not have to be plugged in to the muzzle of the rifle but could be clipped on to the side of the barrel and hence be ready immediately firing was no longer possible. Killiecrankie, which was a victory of sword over musket, was therefore unlikely ever to be imitated.

Killiecrankie has now become a famous beauty spot with a good road running through it. At the time of the battle it was merely a gloomy valley containing a single rough track. The battle itself took place outside the northern end of the pass, but the aftermath occurred in the pass itself along the banks of the Garry. The field where Mackay first stopped his advance is by the main road and is marked by a stone. It is said that he left his baggage here and that this fact saved many lives, for the Highlanders checked their slaughter in order to collect plunder. There is a stone in this field, but it has no inscription; furthermore this road is highly dangerous for motorists to park on. There are other stones which are said to have associations with incidents of the battle but it is difficult to believe in these convenient legends. The 'Soldier's Leap' is authentic. Donald MacBean, one of Mackay's troopers, was pursued by a Highlander who fired a pistol at him. Coming to the water, MacBean found it was about eighteen feet across, but, with a prodigious jump, he cleared it. He survived, and wrote his memoirs. In them he states that the troops fired three volleys in the battle before being overwhelmed; others say they fired only twice.

The visitor's best policy is to visit the National Trust for Scotland Centre on the pass where – as with Bannockburn – the battle is projected on a *tableau vivant*. Here he will be guided to the visitable parts of the battlefield.

# GLENCOE

## 12 February 1692

References to Glencoe usually term it 'The Massacre of Glencoe' and this, unfortunately, is the correct description; it is, however, wrongly thought by many to have been a battle. It appears here so that it may be put into perspective in Scottish history and also that certain prevailing misconceptions about it may be rectified. It also belongs to this account as part of the sequel to Killiecrankie.

After the summer of 1689 public attention and military conflict shifted to Ireland. The deposed James II was already there with money, officers, and arms from France. The ensuing conflict reached its climax in the Battle of the Boyne (1 July 1690), when James's army was defeated by that of William III. Hard and bloody fighting continued until 1692, after which a repressive Irish Parliament had the country firmly held down.

While conflict had been raging over Ireland the situation in Scotland had passed virtually unnoticed. But in the Highlands there were chiefs who had supported Dundee and had fought at Killiecrankie and elsewhere. They were fiercely independent, and in remote areas felt they could continue to be so. Towards the end of 1691 William considered that the best way to establish law and order would be to grant an amnesty and let bygones be bygones. However, a condition of this amnesty was that all the clan chieftains who had not previously done so must acknowledge allegiance by 1 January 1692. All did except Maclan, chief of the Macdonalds of Glencoe. Maclan, partly as a joke and partly to preserve his diminished dignity, put off his submission – which involved taking the oath of allegiance, to the last possible moment. He then went to Fort William – which was not the place appointed for him – and found no magistrate there. His submission therefore could not be made till 6 January. What happened next was inexcusable, though perhaps understandable. The Secretary of State for Scotland was Sir John Dalrymple, Master of Stair, who detested the independent lawlessness of the Highlanders. Dalrymple therefore prevailed on William III to let him make an example of the Macdonalds; he did not, however, tell William that the Macdonalds had already submitted, albeit a few days late.

To understand Dalrymple's action, though not to condone it, it is necessary to have some idea of the Highlands at that time. Highland chiefs had absolute power and would occasionally execute members of the clan whom they felt had deserved the extreme penalty. This was only one aspect of their ancient barbarism; a more irritating one to their more settled neighbours was that they lived only for cattle-raiding and plunder. Many of their more industrious neighbours were paying an annual tribute to save their cattle from being 'lifted' – not always successfully. In the more remote parts of the Highlands it was reported that houses had no chimneys or lights, potatoes were still unknown, iron was too scarce to be used for anything but weapons, and horses dragged carts by their tails. Dalrymple perhaps thought that there was only one lesson such people would understand and it would be the better for the rest of Scotland the sooner it was applied.

The treachery of the massacre, let alone its brutality, appals even now. Dalrymple despatched a regiment, commanded by Campbell of Glenlyon; many of its members came from areas which had experienced the depredations of the Macdonalds. Maclan gave them a traditional Highland welcome, with the best hospitality he could provide; doubtless he thought that this was a part of the ceremonial of oath-taking and allegiance. The glen was full of snow at the time. It says something for Maclan's goodwill that he could entertain a regiment commanded by one of the detested Campbells and not murder him and them; but he did so, and the regiment was with him a fortnight before it struck. At midnight on 12 February, when the Macdonalds were asleep, Campbell gave the order and the massacre began. The Macdonald himself was shot, and thirty-seven others – men, women, and children – were butchered. The remainder scattered into the snowy hills to survive if they could.

Today's visitor will probably visit Glencoe in the summer when the whole area will be strikingly beautiful and peaceful. The massacre took place somewhere between Signal Hill and Aonach Dubh, naturally enough the precise site is not exactly known. By the standards of other massacres, some preceded by battles, this was small indeed. It became notorious for its premeditated treachery, abusing one of the finest traditions of the Highlands – their hospitality – and astonishing all who heard of it by its cold-bloodedness. But, as we have seen above, deplorable though the massacre was it must be seen in the context of place and time. Perhaps the surviving Macdonalds took a grim pride in the fact that a regiment tried to kill a mere 200 men, women, and children, and that even with treachery, surprise and darkness it could only murder less than forty.

# THE BATTLE OF
# PRESTONPANS

# 20 September 1745

At the beginning of the eighteenth century it seemed as if Scotland and England were drawing much closer to each other politically and further wars would be unthinkable. There had, however, been setbacks. In 1698 a Scottish colonial company had set off to colonize the area around Panama, at that time known as Darien. This piece of enterprise was warmly approved by the Scottish Parliament but William III looked coldly on the scheme, refused to confirm its privileges or to give it English backing. The Company, completely surprised by the tropical climate and diseases – for the area was outwardly attractive – had a disastrous experience, and all its settlers died. Appalled by this calamity, the Scots, looking for a cause for the disaster, soon decided that it was due to English envy, inspired by William. So high did feelings run that the Scots began to talk of a separate kingdom again. The Prime Minister, Godolphin, appreciating the dangers of the situation, pressed quickly and strongly for an act of Union to ensure that relations did not deteriorate further. The Bill was passed in 1707. It gave Scotland forty-five members in the House of Commons and sixteen in the Lords. The arms of the two countries were blended by combining the white saltire of St Andrew with the red cross of St George. This became known as the 'Union Jack', a jack being the flag on a ship by which it shows its nationality. Nevertheless, plenty of Scots had doubts about the alleged benefits of this union and the Jacobites lost no opportunities to deplore it. Hope of any positive and successful action was slim, until Queen Anne died in 1714 leaving no direct successor, and George of Hanover, descended from Sophie, daughter of James I, was invited to take the throne. James Stuart, the Old Pretender, the son of the exiled James II, could have had the English throne if he had agreed to become a Protestant, but he refused.

It looked, however, as if the time might be ripe for a Scottish bid for a restoration of the Stuart line. Few English people were pleased at the arrival of an unattractive fifty-four-year-old German who spoke no word of English and had apparently no desire to learn the language of his new subjects. In Scotland dislike of this new king was increased by the fact that he was strongly supported by the Campbell clan; any cause espoused by the Campbells was certain to be detested by their ancient rivals in the Highlands.

In consequence, a rebellion was planned by the Earl of Mar who was soon joined by Gordons, Murrays, Mackintoshes, Macphersons, Farquharsons, Stuarts, and Macdonalds (the last with Glencoe firmly in mind). When this force struck, similar risings were to take place elsewhere, in the Lowlands and on the Border, in Wales and in Devonshire. Unfortunately for the rebels' chances Mar was not the man to lead them, or anybody; he was a somewhat shifty character who had earned the nickname 'Bobbing John'. The risings in Wales and Devonshire were forestalled by swift action on the part of the government, which arrested the local Jacobites before they could put their plans into action. Even so it was a dangerous moment. There were less than 10,000 English troops available, and the rebels looked like putting many more into the field. Furthermore, French support had been promised.

But the 'Fifteen proved a fiasco. With Wales and Devonshire out of the fight, the only hope lay in vigorous action in the north; but vigour, alas, was absent. The northern counties force, under Thomas Forster, a Northumberland squire, was surrounded by a smaller cavalry force and tamely surrendered near Preston, Lancashire. Mar began well by capturing Perth, Aberdeen, and

Dundee, but then halted, leaving Edinburgh and the surrounding area to his opponents. Not until 12 November 1715, two months after he had first raised the standard, did he move south from Perth. The next day he met his opponents at Sherriffmuir, just north of Stirling. The ensuing battle was as curious as it was indecisive. The left wing of each army scattered the opposing right. Then, not knowing whether it had won or lost each army retreated. Mar fell back to Perth, his supporters quarrelling among themselves and each blaming the other for the fact that the army had not managed to force a passage through to England. Even the belated arrival of the Old Pretender himself – a month later – failed to prevent them trickling back to the Highlands. With their hopes and plans in ruins, the leaders also soon went their separate ways. James and certain others went to France, whence no assistance was forthcoming now that Louis xiv was dead. The 'Fifteen, which could have altered history, quietly fizzled out. The rebel army was finally disbanded on 7 February 1716 at Aberdeen. Reprisals were not unduly severe in the conditions of the time. Thirty of the leading figures were hanged and a number were transported, but many kept out of the way and received a pardon later. Many, however, had their estates and property confiscated.

Even less successful was an attempt in 1719. This time three hundred Spanish soldiers were to land in Rossshire where they would find Jacobite allies. Five thousand more Spaniards were to follow. The three hundred landed and were joined by a thousand clansmen under the Marquis of Tullibardine. The five thousand never arrived at all because their transports were all destroyed in a storm. In consequence it was a relatively simple matter for government forces to scatter the insurgents at Glenshiel.

Two important and lasting results followed from these actions.

One was that General Wade, who had been appointed Commander-in-Chief for Scotland built a series of roads, small by modern standards, but large and impressive in their time. These, marked on the map as 'General Wade's military roads' were a ten-year programme which made the Highlands accessible.

although they covered approximately only 250 miles. Not least of their benefits were the bridges which carried them over difficult watercourses.

A second result was the famous Black Watch regiment which was originally raised by Wade as a local police force. The Black Watch subsequently fought as the 42nd, distinguishing itself on the Alma Heights in the Crimea, and on many other battlefields.

After 1719 its English supporters lost interest in the Jacobite cause, but it lived on in Scotland. In 1745 Stuart fortunes suddenly revived, and for a time there was a genuine prospect that a Stuart might once again sit on the English throne. The circumstances were these.

The Old Pretender had two sons. The elder was Charles Edward, the younger Henry (later a Cardinal). Charles Edward was a complete contrast to his unlucky and depressing father. He was cheerful, adventurous, and energetic; he was clearly a born leader, and he looked like a prince of royal blood.

With England heavily involved in a war on the Continent, and thus denuded of troops, 1745 was an obvious time to pick for a bid for power. In the preceding year the French had assembled an invasion fleet at Dunkirk, with every intention of using it, but it had been, once more, destroyed by storms. This was a setback, but Charles was undeterred. He knew in his bones that he could and must win. The battle of Fontenoy on 11 May 1743 confirmed his opinion; the English were now in desperate trouble on the Continent, and all he had to do was to show his face in Scotland and the country would rise to support him

Troubles began early. His little convoy was intercepted at sea and, when he landed in the Outer Hebrides on 2 August 1745, he had only seven supporters with him. On first landing, his reception was daunting, for none of his anticipated supporters wished to join him. He went on to Moidart, gaining a few, and thence to Glenfinnan. At Glenfinnan he raised the standard, declared his father was the rightful King of Scotland, and moved on to Edinburgh.

Glenfinnan had brought him a thousand supporters, and he

was soon joined by another three thousand. With these he moved forward and took Perth. Thence he went to Edinburgh where the city was gained without a fight. It looked – and not only to him – as if success was in his grasp. The best of the English army was overseas and all that could be mustered to meet him was an army of less than three thousand, six battalions in all, of which two were very raw and new. Commanding them was the incompetent Sir John Cope who had already failed to intercept him on the road to Edinburgh. Cope had subsequently embarked his army and landed them at Dunbar, whence he had marched towards Edinburgh. Charles, full of heady triumph, was now moving south – and the two armies met, on 20 September 1745, at Prestonpans, East Lothian.

Cope, who had no alternative but to wait and see what his steadier regiments could do to a Highland charge, deployed his army between Preston Grange and Seaton House. He suspected (rightly) that Prince Charles had artillery and would be relying on traditional weapons. By setting out his troops with their rear to the sea, but not too close, he had arranged that they could not be outflanked; ahead of him lay ditches and hedges which would take the edge off the fiercest and longest charge, he surmised. As the two armies closed, the Highlanders moved on to the higher ground around Tranent and took a long careful look at their opponents. The sight was not encouraging. Knowing their deficiencies in arms, without artillery, and mainly armed with broadsword or makeshift pike, the prospect of a successful charge over rough and unknown ground looked doubtful. Impetuous though they were, they were not suicidal.

Charles Edward, however, was burning for action. He rode restlessly here and there, hoping to hit on a plan which would convince the more cautious of his advisers. Luckily for him he encountered a man named Anderson, who lived near by and was a keen Jacobite. Anderson gave Charles Edward a vital piece of information: it was that a path ran through the bog which was partially protecting Cope's front. If the Young Pretender used this path he could take his whole army round to Cope's eastern flank, where, because of the protection of the bog, the latter's dispositions were thinnest. In the early hours of the next day, long before first light, Charles Edward had taken his army (it numbered only 2,500) along the path and close to Cope's position. At Riggonhead farm they were spotted by one of Cope's outposts and the alarm was given but it was too late for them to be checked here. Cope's army was facing south and the best he could do was to turn it to face east and give battle where the Highlanders chose to offer it. The latter, moving briskly towards the coast at Cockenzie, turned west along the line of the present B6371. Their achievement in crossing such rough country so easily is not now so well appreciated, as the long ditch which could have been such a formidable obstacle has been largely filled in; the presence of a road, a railway track, pylons, and a huge slag heap makes an appreciation of the 1745 terrain difficult though not impossible.

As the sun came up, and shone directly into the eyes of Cope's soldiers, he was still trying to make the best of his new position. On his right he had his artillery, all too close to the Jacobites. Behind were his raw dragoons whose task was to intercept any attack and break it up. Four hundred yards separated the two armies and, as the Jacobites checked their positioning, their whole army was gradually edging forward, closing the gap.

The battle began haphazardly. A range-finding shot from the English line found a target on the Scottish left. A man screamed. It was like a command to the Scots. They had not marched all this way to be picked off at will by the English; now they charged. The fury and impetus surprised even their own leaders. The English gunners got off five rounds and were overwhelmed. The dragoons behind, commanded by Colonel Gardiner, a brave old campaigner, saw the fate of the gunners ahead of them and without waiting for orders decided to avoid it for themselves. Gardiner tried desperately to rally them. Unfortunately they were in an excellent position for a cowardly dash from the battlefield, leaving their comrades in the lurch. On such a small area such a disaster was all too obvious, even to Cope's centre and left, which were now facing the fury of the Highland charge. Here again there was no chance to make use of their muskets before they too were overwhelmed; it was short bayonet against long pike and whirling claymore. Cope's men were like a skilled boxer who is trying to fight off a heavy puncher who is inside his guard. As they reeled back, the Macdonalds on the Highland right, a little late to begin but devastating now they were on the move, swept diagonally into Cope's army crumpling up its left wing as they went.

In minutes the battle was lost, but not over. The remainder of the dragoons also tried to escape but now found their way blocked by fallen or fleeing infantry. The Jacobites too were among them, unhorsing them and slashing them down with claymores. Colonel Gardiner, still fighting, fell with a dozen wounds. Cope made a desperate effort to rally some of the dragoons but the best he could do was to take some 400 men out of battle up the B1349, which was later mockingly christened 'Johnny Cope's road'. Inevitably English losses were as heavy as the Scots were light. Five hundred of Cope's army were killed and another 1,500 taken prisoner. In contrast, the Scots had less than fifty killed and about seventy-five wounded. Much of the slaughter must have taken place where the A198 is crossed by the B1349, for this is where burial pits were found later.

There are various memorials to Prestonpans. There is a large wooden outline of a Highlander and an English soldier, there is a memorial to Col. Gardiner which may be seen from the road, although it is on the other side of the parallel railway line, and there is another monument on the A198 junction immediately behind Cockenzie SSEB Power Station.

# THE BATTLE OF
# CULLODEN

## 18 April 1746

After Bonnie Prince Charlie's devastating victory at Prestonpans it seemed as if not only Scotland but perhaps England too lay at his feet. 'They ran like rabets' he wrote of Prestonpans; clearly his chances were excellent.

Meanwhile, General Wade was sent to Newcastle with ten battalions to fend off the prospective invasion of England. This meant that 10,000 men of a different quality from those he had met before were now facing Charles Edward. Worse was to follow; the Duke of Cumberland was hastily summoned from Flanders with even more veterans, and the militia, lacking in experience but not in dash and courage, was called out.

Foolishly Charles waited five weeks before moving on from Prestonpans. Had he pressed forward at once he might well have reached London. But the delay was fatal, for, although he was rearming and re-equipping, his enemies were making even more strenuous and effective preparations. Even so, when he eventually marched he still had a chance of success, though a diminished one. Sweeping down the western side of England – to avoid Wade's army in Newcastle – he reached Derby. He was now a mere 125 miles from London.

At this moment, the dash and courage which had characterized his enterprise from the moment he landed in Scotland with seven supporters temporarily deserted him. His leading adviser, Lord George Murray, who had been largely responsible for the victory at Prestonpans, considered he was taking too great a risk with

Wade on one side, Cumberland on the other, and an unspecified force of militia also to reckon with. Furthermore he was not getting the recruits he had hoped for, and desertions had reduced his numbers to 3,000. He took advice, and began to retreat; it was now 6 December.

But he was by no means beaten. His nimble Highlanders, although encumbered by plunder, made light work of the snowy road home. Neither Wade nor Cumberland could move fast enough to get near them. Once over the Border Charles paused and took stock. Recruits poured in; his numbers were now back to 10,000. It looked as if he was secure in Scotland at least, even if he had to forgo his visit to Westminster. The view was reinforced at Falkirk, where on 17 January 1746 his army inflicted a sharp and surprising defeat on an English army under General Hawley. Here again a Highland charge at the critical moment was the cause of Jacobite victory.

But now the tide was turning against him. Cumberland had mustered 30,000 men and more were still being called to the colours. Charles could not hope to match such a force, particularly as his army dwindled whenever there were periods of inactivity. His only real hope lay in French intervention. If the French either created a diversion on the southern coast of England or sent a substantial contingent of troops to Scotland, his fortunes could still revive. He was in the extraordinary position of losing a campaign though winning all his battles. But he still had 5,000 men.

Cumberland knew exactly what his task was. At best Prince Charles would have only 6,000 men, and it could well be a thousand less. He could engage these with a picked vanguard and still have superior numbers. He drew off 8,000 of his best troops and with these marched briskly forward after Charles, who was now retreating slowly towards the north-west. By the time he was pressing on to their heels, the Jacobites had had three months of slow retreat, a dispiriting process which had not been helped by shortage of food. Keeping a large army in the field is a hard enough task at the best of times, with its problems of feeding, morale, and supply, but it is doubly difficult in an area with limited supplies of foodstuffs. Nevertheless, cold and hungry though the Jacobites were, they had preserved their morale; after all they had a royal leader who could rough it with the hardest of them and win battles too. They did not know that Cumberland, mindful of the disgraceful defeats at Prestonpans and Falkirk, had been training his army to ensure that such scenes should not be repeated. His men were now thoroughly schooled in the technique of repulsing a Highland charge. The front rank would kneel with fixed bayonets; the rear would fire in volleys. The process employed may still sometimes be seen in ceremonial drill parades today, where it all looks very elegant. In eighteenth-century battle, however, it was entirely purposeful; for after the front rank fired, it would smartly step to the side and rear to reload while the rank from behind stepped forward and went through a similar action. By this means a line of soldiers with loaded muskets was constantly in a position to fire. The kneeling soldiers, after holding their fire till the last agonizing moment, would each lunge with the bayonet to the Highlander on his right front. The bayonet would go in on the Highlanders' unprotected side. This formation and procedure would be a very different matter from the shallow dispositions at Prestonpans. Behind and between the infantry were cannon whose fire would rake the Jacobite lines. Cumberland was probably well aware that, when Cope had arrived back in London after Prestonpans, he had laid bets that the next general sent against the Jacobites would be beaten. Men had laughed at him and accepted his odds. When Hawley was defeated at Falkirk in January, Cope became thousands of pounds richer. Cumberland smiled grimly when he heard of it. He had more than enough troops for his task and had trained them specially; furthermore he knew exactly what his problems were likely to be. Unlike his opponent, Cumberland, the second son of George II, was not a popular leader; he was known to be hasty-tempered, coarse, and tyrannical. He had been outgeneralled at Fontenoy and Lauffelt, but he was a methodical professional and learnt from his own and other people's defeats. He had been appointed commander in Scotland after the dismissal of Hawley. Even so, the full unpleasantness of his character had not yet been revealed.

On 14 April Cumberland reached Nairn. So far Charles's strategy had been to retreat slowly, leading Cumberland's army after him, inflicting a blow here and there, but eventually to lure the English into the hills where the ground would perplex them, the cavalry would be useless, their artillery could not follow, and the whole terrain would be disconcerting. Unfortunately he was completely crippled by lack of money, not merely to pay his troops – who had received nothing for weeks – but even to buy food wherever it might be obtainable. Even the most popular army finds food hard to come by if it has no money to pay for it. Many of Charles's men were now absenting themselves for long or short periods to scrounge for themselves. Morale was not high, for it was thought that the English should have been attacked at river crossings, such as on the Spey. It may have been good strategy to let the redcoats penetrate virtually unmolested right up to the Highlands, but to the Jacobite soldier it made no sense at all.

In fact Charles too had now lost faith in his own strategy. Furthermore he had had enough of retreats. Admittedly, the withdrawal from Derby had been followed by the victory at Falkirk but this retreat had gone on too long. He decided to give battle.

The spot chosen was some rough ground, then known as Drummossie Moor, south-east of Culloden House. There on 15 April the Jacobite army took up position and waited. No English troops appeared. As time wore on the Scots, who were almost starving, took it in turns to creep away and find a few cabbage leaves or – if lucky – a little oatmeal. The staff looked around and appraised the battlefield, which had been reconnoitred and chosen by O'Sullivan the Quartermaster-General. They found it far from satisfactory. It was not rough enough to deter the English cavalry and its very openness made it ideal for English artillery fire. A less suitable site – for Prince Charle's army – could scarcely have been chosen.

Still no English appeared, and by late afternoon a morale-raising plan had been conceived. This was to make a swift night march to Nairn – eight miles away – and deliver a surprise night attack. Highland charges from close quarters in the dark or dawn could well produce a second Prestonpans. Departure was arranged for 7 p.m. But at 7 p.m., when the march was to begin, over a quarter of the army was absent, looking for food. Many refused to return till they had found it; it was decided to leave them behind. Even so, about 4,000 set off in the pitch dark, hungry and sullen, to pick their way through heather, bog, and hillock. Soon the column had straggled and gaps had opened up in it. Lord George Murray was in the van, Prince Charles at the rear. But as Murray approached Cumberland's camp he heard the alarm being raised. Alert sentries must have passed back warning of their approach. Murray, realizing that surprise had been lost and any further move forward would lead to a well-prepared reception, gave the order to retreat. As the rest of the column was still moving forward the confusion may be imagined and it would not have been surprising if Murray's men had been taken for enemy and fired on. However, they were not and for the rest of the night a disconsolate, bewildered, tired, and starving army was trailing back to Culloden. On arrival, dog-tired, they threw themselves on the ground to get some sleep. Prince Charles was as tired as any, but before he lay down himself he organized a final drive to obtain whatever food could be gathered from Inverness. The food was collected but few of his army ever managed to taste it.

Hardly were they asleep when they were roused again. The alarm came from Domhnall Macraonaill Mhic Aillen, Captain of the Men of Glencoe. He was with a party of scouts patrolling the front. 'The redcoats are on us,' he announced.

Charles, pale and hungry, rushed out of his headquarters at Culloden House on hearing the news. He had the recall sounded by a cannon shot, and, as if by a miracle, his followers appeared from bracken, wood, and ditch and fell in in two lines. On the right was the Atholl brigade, commanded by Murray and consisting of Camerons, Stewarts, Macintoshes, Frasers, and a few others. The Camerons thought they were entitled to the place of honour on the extreme right and were not pleased with the dispositions. The centre was commanded by Lord John Drummond and included the Farquharsons; the right had more Stewarts; and the left wing was Macdonald. This line had a few not very reliable guns of varying calibre. The second line contained some cavalry but much of this was now dismounted and serving as infantry. The dispositions extended from Culloden House to Culwinniac farm, and totalled 5,000.

Six hundred yards away Cumberland's army began to take up position. Curiously each army was too preoccupied with its own alignments to pay much attention to the enemy. This, as readers of other books in this series will know, was not an unusual occurrence. Some battles begin as soon as the opponents come within range; others are preceded by hours of waiting or patient manoeuvring. This was one of the latter.

Cumberland's army was deployed in three lines. His front line consisted of Pulteney's, the Royal, Price's, Cholmondeley's, Munro's, and Barrel's regiments, as well as the Royal Scots Fusiliers. The second line was Howard's, Battereau's, Fleming's, Bligh's, Sempill's, Ligonier's, and Wolfe's regiments. Artillery was positioned among the front line, and the cavalry was at the flanks and rear. It numbered 8,000.

Battle began with a burst of Jacobite artillery fire at 1 p.m. Cumberland had ten 3-pounders and they were soon replying. The Jacobite gunners did their best but their guns were poor and badly served; and they had few successes. As the 3-pounders ranged on to them, the Jacobite gun-crews, who were few and inexperienced, ceased firing and abandoned their guns. Still no troops moved. However, after the English artillery had been raking the Highland lines for half an hour, causing severe and increasing casualties, some of Prince Charles's army became restless. It was hardly surprising. Without food or sleep they had been required to stand for over four hours and now they were being steadily slaughtered by the English artillery. Charles, who had positioned himself at the rear, but not for lack of courage, was unaware of what was happening. Soon, however, he began to receive urgent requests for battle orders.

At 1.30 he at last gave the command to attack. The word passed along the line, but the Macdonalds, mortally affronted because they were on the left instead of the right of the line refused to move immediately. But others did. As they surged forward on to the cannon and muskets, fearful gaps appeared in their lines but they never hesitated. They covered the ground faster than anticipated and it was as well for the English infantry that they had kept their powder dry in spite of the rain, which was blowing hard into the Jacobite faces. Incredibly, all the old Highland magic was still there. Battered, starved, exhausted, the Prince's army, who were by no means all Highlanders, went into the charge as if they were fresh troops. Opposite were certain English regiments whose reputation had taken hard knocks in recent battles, and even earlier ones. This time, whatever happened, win or lose, they swore, they would not be disgraced. As the Jacobites came hurtling in the redcoats poured volley after volley at them. At once this had become a battle of heroes. Nobody in his senses could have predicted that the Scots would reach this far; nobody in his right mind would have dared speculate that, if they did, the English could hold them on their bayonets. The scene was unbelievable. Men were fighting on with half a dozen wounds, perhaps with an arm already lopped off, but slashing out with the other before they fell. It was, however, in the long run, a victory for the musket. By the time the regiments were hand-to-hand, the English had too great a numerical advantage to lose – unless a miracle occurred. Even so, neither army was fully committed; some Scots had never come into position, and the English reserve had scarcely been touched. But those who were committed fought with a frenzy and endurance that was almost superhuman. And in an hour it was all over.

The aftermath of this battle is perhaps too well known to need description here. Prince Charles escaped, and, with a price of

£30,000 on his head, hid in the Western Highlands before he obtained a ship for France. Not a man attempted to betray him. He died in 1788. When his brother Henry died in 1807, the male Stuart line became extinct.

The sequel to Culloden was barbarous. Cumberland earned the nickname 'the Butcher' from the atrocities he unloosed on the Highlands, and the English Government which followed his cruelties with repressive measures were equally at fault. Cumberland's troops mercilessly hunted down the fugitives, dragging them out of cottages where they had found refuge and shooting them in cold blood. Equally brutal was the treatment of those suspected of aiding the escape of Prince Charles. It was entirely inexcusable even after the scare that the '45 had given to the English. Cumberland's attitude may perhaps be understood. He did not see the Scots as opponents such as the French to whom one might lose without great loss. He saw the Scots as a potential danger which might erupt again and destroy him and his line utterly. This he was determined to prevent. But no one, Scottish or English, will ever forgive or excuse him.

Much of the battlefield is now wooded over, but there is one clear strip from which the scene in 1746 may be visualized. It is now National Trust property and well signposted and preserved.

# Index

(Roman numerals in italic refer to the maps)

Abercorn 91
Albany, Duke of 82, 87, 88
Alford 117
Alnwick 90, 92
Ancrum Moor, the Battle of (1545) 99–103, *VII*
Angus, Earl of 55, 92, 100, 109
Arran, Earl of 100, 108
Atholl, Marquis of 130–1

Baillie, General 117–19
Balliol, Edward 69–70, 73
    crowned King 72
Balliol, John 47, 59, 69
Bannockburn, Battle of (1314) 59–67, 72, *III*
Beaton, Cardinal 99
Beck, Antony de
    *see* Durham, Bishop of
Bendar 84
Berwick 52, 66, 70, 72, 73, 77, 93
Black Watch, The 144
Bohun, Sir Henry de 64, 65
Bohun, Humphrey de
    *see* Hereford, Earl of
Border Warfare 87–98
Borestone, The 64, 66
Bothwell Bridge, Battle of (1679) 130
Bothwell, Earl of 99, 106
Boyne, Battle of (1690) 137
Bruce, Edward 61, 62–6
    crowned King of Ireland 69
    death of 69

Bruce, Robert 59–66
    death of 69

Campbell of Glenlyon 138–9
Charles I, King of England 114, 117, 125
Charles Edward (Bonnie Prince Charlie) 144–6, 149, 150, 152–5
Coldringham, siege at 98
Coldstream Castle 95
Comyn, John 56, 57, 59–60
Conway, Lord 115–16
Cope, Sir John 145–7, 151
Covenanters 114, 118, 123, 130
Cressingham 47, 48, 51–2
Cromwell, Oliver 125, 129
Culloden, Battle of (1646) 149–56, *XVI*
Cumberland, Duke of 149–55

Dalhousie, Ramsay of 51, 84
Dalrymple, Sir John 138
Darnley, Lord Henry 95, 99
Dirleton Castle 54
Donald, Earl of Mar 70
Douglas, Sir Archibald 71
    became Regent 70
    death of 72
Douglas Castle 91
Douglas, Commander of Scots Right Wing 76
Douglas, Earl of 82
    murdered 89
Douglas, Earl of 90

Douglas, Earl of (1455) 92, 93
Douglas, Sir James (Black Douglas) 66, 69
Douglas, Sir William 66
  death of 70
Drummossie Moor 152
Dumbarton 88
Dumfries 89
Dunbar, Battle of (1650) 64, 125-8, XII
Dunbar Castle 82, 89
Dundaff, Grahame of 51
  death of 56
Dundee Castle 49
Dundee, Viscount 130-3, 137
Duns 71
Durham, Bishop of 54

Edinburgh Castle 61, 92, 107, 125, 131
Edward I, King of England 47-8, 53-7, 59, 60
  death of 60
Edward II, King of England 60-2, 65-7
  murder of 69
Edward III, King of England 69-74, 77
Edward IV, King of England 91-2
Edward VI, King of England 105
Evers, Sir Ralph 100
  death of 103

Falkirk, Battle of (1298) 53-7, 59, II
Falside Hill (Fawside Hill) 107, 108
Flodden, Battle of 97
Fontenoy, Battle of (1743) 144

Gillies Hill 64, 66
Glencoe, Massacre at (1692) 137-9, XIV
Glendower, Owen 81
Gloucester, Earl of 66
Graham, Colonel John of Claverhouse
  see Dundee, Viscount
Grey, Lord 106-7, 109

Halidon Hill, Battle of (1333) 69-72, IV
Harlaw, Battle of 88
Hawley, General 150-1
Hedgeley Moor, Battle of 92
Henry IV, King of England 81, 82
  at Battle of Towton 91
Henry VI, King of England 92
Henry VII, King of England 94
Henry VIII, King of England 96, 99
  death of 105
Hereford, Earl of 54, 56, 64
  see also Bohun, Humphrey de
Hereford, Earl of 99-100
Hertford, Earl of
  see Seymour, Edward
Hexham, Battle of 92
Highlanders 109, 119, 121, 127, 133, 134, 145
Homildon Hill, Battle of (1402) 81-5, VI
Humbleton Hill
  see Homildon Hill, Battle of 83

'Ill Raid', The 97

James I, King of Scotland 88
  murder of 89

James II, King of Scotland 89, 90
  death of 91
James III, King of Scotland 92
  murder of 93
James IV, King of Scotland 93-6
  death of 97
James V, King of Scotland 98
James VI, King of Scotland and
  James I, King of England 96
James II, King of England 130,
  137
Jedburgh Castle 87, 97, 100

Ker, Sir Robert 96
Killiecrankie, Battle of (1689)
  129-35, XIII
Kilsyth, Battle of (1645) 117-19,
  X
Knox, John 113-14

Lamberton, Bishop 57, 59
Lauder 92
Layton, Sir George 103
Lennox, Earl of 88
Leslie, Sir Alexander of Balgonie
  115
Leslie, Sir David, Major-General
  122, 126-7
Leven, Lord 122
Lindores, Abbey of 93
Loudon Hill, Battle of 60
Lowlanders 109, 121

Mackay, General Hugh 130-3
Maclan of Glencoe 137-8
Mar, Earl of 70, 142
March, Earl of 82, 83
Mary, Queen of Scots 95, 98, 111
  death of 99

Methven, Battle of 60
Montrose, Marquis of 115, 117-21
Moray, Sir Andrew 70
Mowbray, Sir Philip de 61, 66
Mytton-on-Swale 66

Naseby, Battle of 117
Nesbit Moor 82
Newburn, Battle of (1840) 113-
  16, IX
Newburn Ford, Rout of 116
Newcastle 82-3
Neville's Cross, Battle of (1346)
  73-9, 87, V
Norham Castle 95
Northumberland, Earl of 114

Ogle, Sir Robert 89
Ormsby 47, 48

Palace Hill 101
Pembroke, Earl of 60
Penrith 87
Percy, 3rd Earl of Northumber-
  land 90
Percy, Harry (Hotspur) 83
  killed at Battle of Shrewsbury
  85
Philiphaugh, Battle of 121
Pinkie, Battle of (1574) 105-111,
  VIII
Prestonpans, Battle of (1745)
  141-7, XV

Randolph, Earl of Moray 66
  became Regent 69
  death of 70
Red Riggs 84
Renfrew 61, 91

Richard II, King of England 79
    murder of 81
Richard III, King of Scotland 82
Rothesay, Duke of 82
Roxburgh, Castle 52, 61, 70, 88,
    91

Sauchieburn, Battle of 93
Salisbury, Earl of 89
Scott, Sir Walter 100
Selkirk 97, 122
Seton, Sir Andrew 71
Seton, Thomas 71
Seymour, Edward 105, 107-8
Shrewsbury, Battle of 84
Slain Man's Lee 123
Somerset, Duke of
    see Seymour, Edward
Stirling 54, 62-3
    Castle 61, 65, 66
Stirling Bridge, Battle of 47-52,
    55, 1
Stewart, Alexander 88
Stewart, Murdoch 83, 84

Stewart, Patrick 131
Strathavon Castle 91
Surrey, Earl of 95, 97

Tantollon, siege at 98
Tippermuir, Battle of 117
Towton, Battle of (1461) 91
Twenge, Sir Marmaduke 51

Umphraville 87

Vane, Sir Ralph 106
Vane, Sir George 107

Wade, General 143, 149-50
Wallace, William 48-56, 59
    death of 57
Warbeck, Perkin 95
Warenne, John de 47-52, 64
Warkworth 90
Warwick 108, 110
William III, King of England
    130, 141
Wood, Sir Andrew 94